Foreword

First and foremost, I want to give all glory to the Father, Son, and Holy Spirit.

I am Michael Driver, I graduated from Arlington Baptist College, and I am a Preacher and Teacher of the Gospel of Christ.

I am so grateful that the Lord allowed me to meet and listen to Robert's testimony about the little glimpse of Heaven he saw. I had the honor and privilege to listen to this man pour out his heart and speak of the experience he had, which blew me away.

As a theological student, I was very skeptical when I first encountered Robert. I had many thoughts: Is this man for real? What is his agenda? Is he coming with a "New Gospel"? But after this precious brother in Christ started to reveal the things he saw, heard, and witnessed; I knew I was in for something special. I want to also make known that Robert is a born-again Christian filled with the Holy Spirit, and his love for Jesus is so comforting and heartfelt.

The book that Robert has been commissioned to write by Jesus is not a book explaining new doctrines or trying to convince you of something that would scare you; rather, this book is a glimpse of the precious and wonderful experiences that Jesus allowed him to have. Robert's testimony is something that I believe everyone should hear. He gives an account of what he saw and who he got to speak with while he was in heaven for 44 hours.

The vibrant and colorful revelation of Heaven is something that I believe all believers think about in their lifetime. What do the trees and waters look like? Are there animals in heaven? What do you smell, and what is the feeling that you feel while you are there? These are some of the questions that have been asked by people, and he has a wonderful response.

My hope is that all people will have the opportunity to read this testimony, and I pray that God will fill your soul and spirit with joy, tears, and hope.

1 Corinthians 2:6-13 (NASB)

Yet we do speak wisdom among those who are mature; a wisdom, however, not of this age nor of the rulers of this age, who are passing away; but we speak God's wisdom in a mystery, the hidden wisdom which God predestined before the ages to our glory; the wisdom which none of the rulers of this age has understood; for if they had understood it they would not have crucified the Lord of glory; but just as it is written,

"THINGS WHICH EYE HAS NOT SEEN AND EAR HAS NOT HEARD, AND WHICH HAVE NOT ENTERED THE HEART OF MAN, ALL THAT GOD HAS PREPARED FOR THOSE WHO LOVE HIM."

For to us God revealed them through the Spirit; for the Spirit searches all things, even the depths of God. For who among men knows the thoughts of a man except the spirit of the man which is in him? Even so the thoughts of God no one knows except the Spirit of God. Now we have received, not the spirit of the world, but the Spirit who is from God, so that we may know the things freely given to us by God, which things we also speak, not in words taught by human wisdom, but in those taught by the Spirit, combining spiritual thoughts with spiritual words.

Michael Driver
Graduate from Arlington Baptist College
Preacher and Teacher of the Gospel of Christ

44 HOURS
IN HEAVEN

ROBERT MARSHALL

Foreward by Michael Driver

Table of Contents

www. 44HoursInHeaven.org
www.44HoursInHeaven.com
Robert@44HoursInHeaven.org

44 Hours in Heaven

Chapter 1
Prologue

Let me begin by saying that I am not an author. I have never authored a book. I'm not a preacher or a pastor, and I'm certainly not a Bible scholar.

Like most people, I never thought I was a bad person, but I certainly was not the greatest person either. I am, like most people, a regular guy. I had my selfish moments, and at times I was self-serving. Multiple times, my decisions were based on what was good for me. I always listened to the radio station, WIIFM: "What's In It For ME"!

What would I get out of it? I do not mean that I only thought of myself, but even when I would give a compliment, it was in the back of my mind that they would think I was a good person. So, my actions were self-serving. I just did not have the right motivations.

For most of my life, I was ambivalent and mostly ignorant about the things of God. I went through life with continuous blessings from God and I looked at them as simply good fortune.

My life has been good. I was enjoying retirement life, but never once did I think that I would die 3 times on May 19th, 2024. I certainly did not think God would bring me back from death once, let alone three times. And never did I think I would visit heaven each of those times.

I also never thought that I would be the one who was seeing the love and purity of Jesus. I never thought I would be involved in spreading God's word and love. Yet now I know that I am, and I am blessed to do so.

While in the United States Army I spent multiple tours of duty in a war zone in Vietnam. During that time there were many occasions I should have died in combat. I received a few medals for valor, including the Silver Star and Purple Hearts for wounds received in combat, and a few others for valor.

All of which I chalked up to as being in the wrong place at the right time or in the right place at the wrong time; either way, I looked at it as luck. Now, I know luck had nothing to do with it. It was God watching out for me then and throughout my life.

I am 75 years old. Only God knew His plan for my life, that He had a purpose for me in this life.

Most often we do not pay attention to day-to-day events, successes, and failures because those mundane events don't fit into what we think our life should be. We want to be in control of everything in our lives, family, work, friends, and children. I know that was the case for me.

I wanted to be in control of everything. Many considered me arrogant and very controlling. I did not want to turn control over to anybody, not even GOD!

However, now I have come to realize that we need to let God be in control and allow Him to guide us in all that we do. In Isaiah 55:8 (NIV), God tells us **"For my thoughts are not your thoughts, neither are your ways my ways." Declares the LORD.**

God is with us every moment of every day, watching out for each one of us. I know without a doubt He loves us and desires us to love Him and give our life to Him. He wants us to willingly come to him with an open mind and heart and accept him as our Lord and Savior.

If we do, then He will send an advocate, the Holy Spirit, who guides and helps us understand and follow God's guidance until the day we are all brought together in heaven where we will live with Him for all eternity.

For reasons that are beyond my understanding, other than the love and grace of God, I was given the blessing to survive all I went through in war and my life until May 2024, when I died and came back from the dead not once, not twice, but three times. The only thing that I can attest this to is the miracle of the love and grace of God.

God chose to perform this miracle on May 19th, 2024, when he allowed me to die and enter Heaven.

I met Jesus face-to-face. Jesus took me by my hand as we walked through Heaven and He showed many things to me.

As we walked, he shared and explained a multitude of truths about Heaven and Earth. He also gave me an understanding of what was written in the Bible, as well as why it was written and how we are to apply it in our lives.

I was given a glimpse of how beautiful and peaceful Heaven is and how caring, warm, and loving God is. Each time I died, I went to Heaven, and I was surrounded by the warmth and love of Jesus.

The insight into Heaven, the lessons Jesus shared with me, and the personal glimpse of Heaven was, and is still, a humbling reminder of God's love and unmerited favor.

God's grace is often defined as unmerited favor, kindness, and mercy of God. It is God's freely given, undeserved love, comfort, and care of humanity particularly in the context of salvation and forgiveness of sins.

I cannot answer why God chose to bless me with unmerited miracles, but I can say that I am humbled and honored to be able to testify about God's miracles and His assurance that He is alive and continuing to perform miracles today.

My hope and prayers are that as you read the following account of how I died three times, entered Heaven three times, and returned to life on Earth, you will discover the love and power of Jesus. I am writing this book with the love of Jesus inside me, as well as the knowledge and lessons Jesus shared and blessed me with while I was with Him in Heaven.

My hope is that you will discover an assurance that Jesus and Heaven are real. I also pray that you will accept the truth and believe that Jesus died on the cross and rose from the dead for our sins and Jesus now sits at the side of the Father. Jesus paid the ultimate price so that we could be forgiven and spend all of eternity in Heaven with Him.

If you do accept Jesus, you too will be able to look forward to one day being able to see what I saw, what I experienced, and a lot more. You will be able to experience the love of Jesus and the gift of eternal life in the presence of Jesus Christ Himself.

Each time I share the account of my experience of going to heaven and returning, it brings me to tears of love and appreciation for the blessings I experienced. It is the most miraculous experience and blessing I have ever received.

It still baffles me that this happened to me, rather than to some more qualified person. There are so many people who have dedicated their lives to serving God and witnessing for God. Yet, as I write this, I realize again that Jesus chose me an ordinary person, to witness for Him. God loves us and hopes we all accept Him completely.

After dying and going to Heaven and meeting Jesus face to face, I realized I needed to make some major changes in my life and allow Jesus to be in control.

You see we are all the same. We all were born into sin, and we think that if we do good things, God will see our efforts and that will make Him happy, and that good works will get us into Heaven. However, it is not by works; it is not by virtuous deeds but by faith in His love and His grace. (**John 3:16 NIV**) "**For God so loved the world** that He gave His one and only Son, that whoever believes in him shall not perish but have eternal life."

In the following chapters, I will try my best to give an accurate account of my dying and each trip to Heaven so that you may experience the love of God and His miracles through me. Also, I will share questions from people with whom I have shared my testimony of dying and my meeting with Jesus face-to-face and the answers to those questions.

Chapter 2

Death 3 Times

I died three times on the same day. The first time I died was for 15 minutes as a result of suffocation from my airway being blocked by a mass in my neck, and cardiac arrest; the second time was approximately 20 minutes as a result of bleeding into my lungs and drowning in my blood caused by the doctors surgically performing a cricothyroidotomy to create an airway and a second subsequent cardiac arrest; the third time I died was for approximately 55 minutes because of oxygen deprivation, stress, and a third subsequent cardiac arrest. I was dead due to cardiac arrest and oxygen deprivation for a total of approximately 90 minutes.

Each time my heart stopped; CPR was performed to attempt to restart my heart. The result of dying was devastating to my brain, body, and organs.

There are multiple physical effects of dying from oxygen deprivation. The heart stops beating, the brain stops functioning, and other vital organs, including the kidneys and liver, stop all activity. All the body systems powered by these organs shut down, they can no longer continue the ongoing processes viable for life.

The time with oxygen deprivation is critical because of the fragile balance between life and death hinging on the brain's vital need for oxygen, which, when disrupted, can cause a multitude of life-devastating consequences. Without an oxygen supply, the intricate network of neurons that form thoughts, memories, and the very essence of life begins to falter, potentially leading to irreversible damage or death.

My heart stopped three times. Indicating a "flatline" each time I died. My brain was oxygen-deprived, and brain activity ceased.

While in the ICU, the healthcare providers determined that I was unresponsive because there was no evidence of visual, auditory, or tactile stimulation. I was unresponsive to all stimuli, including pain. I lost my reflexes, such as the gag and cough reflex, and my pupils remained fixed and unresponsive to light; I was unable to breathe without the support of a respirator.

My brain could not tell my heart to beat, my lungs to breathe, or any other bodily functions. Without a ventilator and mechanical stimulation, my body would cease all activity and could not function. I was brain-dead!

As one of the doctors told me afterward when I went back to visit the ICU where I had died, they can fix a lot of things physically; they could even replace organs like hearts, kidneys, etc., but they have never been, nor were they ever able to repair or replace a brain that had been damaged or died.

My first trip to Heaven lasted 15 minutes, the second trip lasted 17 minutes, and the third trip was 43 hours and 28 minutes. There is no way to measure time in Heaven. The time I am referring to that I was in

Heaven is noted in the medical record as the time I was unresponsive to all stimuli. Heaven exists without days, hours, or years.

Chapter 3

My Visit To A Local Emergency Room In Willow Park, Texas
May 16, 2024

On Thursday, May 16, 2024, I woke up not feeling well. I had a sore throat and an earache. I thought it may have been the beginning of the flu and, as with most viruses, would pass, but I could not have been more wrong.

As the day progressed, so did my condition. I thought just to be safe I would go to the local emergency room and ask to be evaluated for COVID. When I arrived at the small, free-standing emergency room, the nurse took me to an examination room, where I waited for a doctor.

After the usual preliminary exams, the doctor entered the room and completed the more focused peripheral exam. After examining me, he said, "I am concerned about the swelling on the left side of your neck; I am ordering a COVID test and blood for lab tests, along with a CT scan to take a look at that bulge on your neck."

Once the tests were completed, he returned. He positioned himself on the physician's stool at the end of the exam room. He looked straight at me and said, "I am going to give it to you straight." I felt the hair on the back of my neck bristle as I became apprehensive by his directness and the concerned look on his face.

The doctor said, "First of all you do not have COVID." I thought, "Whew, that's a relief."

Then, he continued, "I found some abnormalities on the CT scan." He explained that he had sent my CT scan to two other doctors for their opinions and whether they could confirm his findings.

He said, "I have conferred with the other two doctors, and we all agree that this may indicate a new cancer diagnosis. It could be an infection, but they also mentioned cancer."

The doctor explained that because of the aggressive nature of the mass in my neck, combined with my blood test results, he was 99 percent certain the mass on the CT scan was cancer. The doctor went on to say, "I recommend you follow up immediately with an ENT surgeon. "I am also going to order a course of antibiotics and steroids and treat you as if you have an infection and also add a dose of dexamethasone as well." He also said he had spoken with an ENT surgeon who treats throat cancer and recommended I see him as soon as possible. The sooner, the better. He was emphatic that I not delay the appointment and that if the ENT could squeeze me in on Monday take that appointment. He then gave me the ENT surgeon's card to set the appointment.

I left the emergency room clutching the business card of a physician who would start treatment for an aggressive form of cancer. I do not remember driving home, but I somehow found myself in the driveway trying to formulate how to tell Carol about my diagnosis.

I decided that direct and kind were my best options. When I entered my house, Carol was standing in the kitchen, and she asked what the doctor said. I replied with, "Baby Doll, the doctor thinks I may have cancer." That seemed to be cruel, but I could not think of a kinder way to deliver the news.

When I dropped that bombshell, Carol turned to me and let me know she thought that was nothing to joke about. My reply was, "I would not joke about something like that."

Carol said she had two choices, freak out or take a breath and deal with the news with supportive determination. She decided on the latter since freaking out would do more harm than good, and it would not change the diagnosis.

"Alrighty then, what do we need to do next?" was Carol's first response in what I thought was a straight and calm voice. My reply included the plan for an immediate appointment on Monday with the ENT recommended by the physician at the ER. I was never able to make or keep that appointment!

Chapter 4
Admission To The Fort Worth Hospital
1st Death

The following day, May 17th, Carol and I went to a coin show in a neighboring town. Around 2:00, while driving home from the coin show, I admitted that we hadn't eaten all day and I felt hungry, so we stopped for a quick bite. But when I took the first bite, I found that I could not swallow, even the drink would not go down.

As a Speech Language Pathologist, Carol knew this sudden inability to swallow could be profoundly serious. We immediately rushed to the emergency room at the main hospital in downtown Fort Worth.

Upon entering the emergency room, the admission staff quickly observed the medical emergency: I was having difficulty breathing. I was immediately escorted to the care area of the ER and met with a member of the medical team who performed the perfunctory vital signs and symptom identification.

The hospital staff responded to my symptoms and ordered a new CT scan and a broader, all-encompassing blood test. The results showed I had **"unstable/abnormal vital signs and life-threatening conditions**," as described in my medical record. I was at risk of my airway being blocked by the mass indicated on the CT scan and I needed emergency intubation with ventilator support. They moved me to a surgical suite, inserted the oral intubation tube, and admitted me to the ICU immediately.

Emergency Room Medical Note:

IMPRESSION:

Increased inflammatory change in the deep left neck soft tissues with worsening swelling of the epiglottis and moderate to severe airway narrowing. Additional inflammatory change involving the left submandibular fossa and submandibular gland as well as the left anterior belly of the digastric. Findings suggest worsening infectious pharyngitis/tonsillitis/epiglottitis. No drainable collection.

Left glossotonsillar sulcus fullness persists. Although superimposed infection is likely, evaluation for an underlying malignancy should be pursued. Direct visualization and tissue sampling may be warranted by ENT. Follow-up CT neck with contrast in one to 3 months is recommended to confirm resolution.

No cervical lymphadenopathy by size criteria.

Incidental severe spinal canal narrowing C5-6 due to ossification of the posterior longitudinal ligament.

For the next two days, I rested comfortably, my body fighting the infection with the help of IV antibiotics, and the intubation tube that kept the mass away from my airway.

On Sunday, May 19th, around 2 pm, my lab results and respirations showed improvement; according to the entries from the emergency room physician, if the white blood cell count improved and the patient had good oxygen saturation, the oral tracheostomy tube could be removed. So, the physician on duty, responding to the medical record, read my lab reports, checked my oxygen levels, and, being satisfied that my condition had improved sufficiently, planned to remove my oral tracheostomy tube to allow me to breathe on my own.

The physician was accompanied by a nurse to deliver the good news; my condition had improved sufficiently to remove the oral tracheostomy tube. She explained to Carol that the sedation would be reduced to make sure that I could breathe independently, and once that happened, the tube could be removed.

From the ICU Medical Record:

> *Patient has not seen a speech pathologist or GI doctor officially. Patient reportedly was having increasing pain of the left side of his neck where the sensitivity caused him to have difficulty even wearing collars or the seat belt. Patient reportedly has had no fevers or chills.*
>
> *Patient was recently seen at another ER yesterday and was given steroids and antibiotics to take.*
>
> *Despite this patient had clinical worsening and upon presentation was identified to have severe*

narrowing of the airway and received an
intubation with the anesthesia. Patient does have
a cuff leak at the time of presentation.

When the decrease in sedation afforded me the
chance to be awake enough to see Carol, my spirits
lifted, and I was feeling better. Carol explained that over
the past two days, I had been sedated but that the
medications had worked, the infection had improved,
and they would be in to remove the oral tracheostomy
tube.

I felt a wave of relief pour over me; we had
made the right decision to come to the hospital; they
saved my life. The thought occurred to me that had I
gone to bed at home after the coin show, I might have
lost the ability to breathe in the middle of the night. That
could have been a devastating decision.

Finally, the doctor and nurse arrived at my
bedside to remove the tracheostomy tube. My spirits
were high, and Carol was excited. Carol stepped out of
the room for the actual removal procedure, but once they
completed the treatment, she joined me in the room. All
four of us were in great spirits; I was going to be just
fine. A course of antibiotics and fluid, and I would have
my ticket to go home.

Everything seemed fine for a while, so the
doctor and nurse left my room to look after other
patients in the ICU.

It was about 30-40 minutes after the physician removed my oral tracheostomy tube. Carol, who just moments ago was in good spirits because they pulled my oral trach tube allowing me to breathe on my own, returned to my room. to discover me lifeless and blue.

Carol ran through the ICU room door and yelled, "Come quick, he is blue!" The doctor was a few feet away, consulting with the nurse. She ran immediately to my bedside, and the nurse pulled the code blue button. I was in distress and blue, absent any airway movement, and I had suffered a cardiac arrest; I was unresponsive. I died!

> Physician's Progress note from May 19, 2024
> *About 30-40 minutes after extubation, wife ran to me in the ICU and said "he is blue" I presented immediately to the bedside and nursing pulled a code blue button. He was arrested, found to be blue without any airway movement., and CPR was started. I grabbed the bronchoscopy and prepared for intubation but given his airway history this admission a "failed airway team" was called. Shortly thereafter both anesthesia and trauma surgery presented to the bedside. With assistance of anesthesia two attempts were made at intubation through the vocal cords but were unsuccessful. Due to this proceeding with emergency cricothyrotomy but trauma surgery was started.*

Sometime during those 30 to 40 minutes, without

warning, the mass in my neck ballooned over my airway. The result of this blockage was complete oxygen deprivation; my breathing stopped, and the indicator on the monitor measuring my heart showed a flatline, I was in cardiac arrest. I had suffocated to death. As the minutes passed while I lay there dead, a precious fleeting stretch of time created oxygen deprivation and heart stoppage that resulted in a cataclysmic timeline of my brain cells dying, and my imminent death.

It was now a reality. I was clinically dead with no heartbeat, brain activity, or oxygen, the likelihood of resuscitation and survival after 15 minutes is impossible.

According to all leading medical facilities, medical facts, and knowledge, the brain uses up to one-fifth of the body's oxygen supply, to send nerve signals throughout the body and produce energy. Without oxygen, the brain and vital organs cannot survive. very long.

When the brain is deprived of oxygen for as little as five minutes, brain cells begin-to die, which leads to irreversible brain damage or death. Brain cells start to die within 30 seconds of low oxygen levels.

When the oxygen supply stops, brain hypoxia rapidly causes severe brain damage or death. Brain damage occurs when oxygen saturation drops below 80%; Brain cells are sensitive to lack of oxygen, and brain cells start dying within 30 seconds.

Brain death can occur as soon as four to six minutes after the brain stops receiving oxygen. This process is known as apoptosis. Recovery from brain death is impossible.

In general, and according to all leading medical experts, medical facilities, and medical research, the brain cannot survive without oxygen for very long.

- **Between 30-180 seconds of oxygen deprivation,** you may lose consciousness.
- **At the one-minute mark,** brain cells begin to die.
- **At three minutes,** neurons suffer more extensive damage and lasting brain damage becomes more likely.
- **At five minutes,** death becomes imminent.
- **At 10 minutes,** even if the brain remains alive, a coma and lasting brain damage are inevitable.
- **At 15 minutes,** survival becomes impossible.

Chapter 5
Carol's Point Of View: My Life Changed

Robert woke up the morning of May 16, 2024, complaining of a sore throat and earache. I thought it was probably "swimmer's ear" related to water in his ear from a recent shower. I told him to put the heating pad on it and try to get the area to relax and open the area to let the water escape. He got the heating pad but said the area was too sore to touch and put the heating pad away. I thought he was likely brewing some sort of infection, and thought he was probably coming down with a viral or bacterial infection.

The next morning, he wasn't any better, and he decided to go to the local free-standing emergency room. I wanted to go with him, but I couldn't go with him due to a zoom meeting scheduled a few days prior. I couldn't skip it because I was central to the topic of the meeting.

He came home from seeing the physicians in the ER and calmly stated that the physicians ran several tests, including a CAT scan, and told him it was either an infection or, most likely, a rapidly advancing form of neck cancer.

That information sent shock waves through every nerve in my body. My career has been on the fringes of the healthcare system, working as a Speech Language Pathologist, I have seen patients with treatment for neck cancer and was aware of what we may be facing. So, with that information, I had two choices: Freak out or stay calm and address the circumstances as they arise. I chose the latter because, in my way of thinking, freaking out doesn't solve any problems; it makes new ones.

The next day Saturday, we went about our plans and attended a coin show in a neighboring city. We were there for about 45 minutes when he decided he'd had enough and still wasn't feeling his usual self.

On the way home he drove through a fast-food restaurant to "grab a bite". He took his first bite, and spat it into the bag, stating he couldn't swallow. I encouraged him to try the soda, it went down, but it took two attempts for him to swallow the entire first gulp. My experience told me we had an emergency, and we needed to get to the emergency room right away.

We traveled home, dropped off our coin collection, and immediately started the 45-minute drive to the main hospital in downtown Fort Worth. By this time, he didn't feel safe driving, and his breathing was a little more strident, so I drove.

I dropped him off at the emergency room entrance and parked the car. By the time I entered the emergency room lobby, he was already being treated in the treatment area. The triage physician ordered the tests, and within minutes, the treating Pulmonologist was sitting in front of us and telling us his plan to intubate him to save his airway from completely closing.

I was beginning to understand the dire situation he was facing. The Pulmonologist believed the reason for the need to protect the airway was due to a mass on the left side of the larynx with a rapidly growing infection. He ordered Robert to the emergency treatment room, where he was sedated, intubated, and placed with IV fluids and an IV antibiotic.

He was moved to the Intensive Care Unit, with plans to monitor him until Monday when a more intensive and aggressive care plan would be developed pending the effectiveness of antibiotics.

By the time he was situated in the ICU, it was after midnight, and I took the long, lonely 45-minute drive from the hospital to our home.

I woke early that Saturday morning and left for the hospital around 8 a.m. to be near him and check on his progress. He was heavily sedated, resting well, and appeared comfortable. I visited with the nurse and the physician on the floor and had confidence he was receiving excellent care. Even though he didn't know I was there because he was heavily sedated. I stayed until early evening, planning on returning the next day.

My parting instructions to the care team were to call me throughout the night if there were any changes and I would keep my phone next to the bed.

Sunday morning, I again left around 8:00 to be in the hospital with Robert and check on the progress of the antibiotics. I visited with the nurses, and he was resting peacefully under sedation.

Around 10:00, I met with the physician, who explained his lab results were very promising, and that he was making excellent progress. Her plan was to lower his sedation and remove the oral intubation tube that afternoon. You can imagine my relief, the crisis averted!

Once the physician began decreasing the sedation, I took the time to thank God by finding a secluded area of the hospital outside on a patio. Peace enveloped me as I prayed for thankfulness and guidance for the coming days.

I returned to the ICU to anxiously await Robert's return to consciousness and road to recovery.

Around 2:00 Robert was awake and noticed me at his bedside. Gripping his hand, I told him the plan was to remove the troublesome tube in his mouth and rejoice in God's rapid healing. Soon enough, the physician entered the room with her nurse and explained the procedure to Robert and me and laid out her expectations for his response.

I left the room, not wanting to see the procedure as it might leave an unpleasant lasting memory in my mind.

I came back when the nurse and doctor told me, "All clear; he is doing fine." Without the trach tube in his throat, he was able to whisper a few words. The nurse had given him a suction wand to suction saliva should he not feel comfortable swallowing; after all, a tube in your throat could cause a painful reaction when it is removed.

Robert was in great spirits after I explained all that had happened. He nodded to the nurse and doctor who were encouraged to see him breathing on his own. They stayed in the room for about 30 minutes, checking his oxygen saturation, pain, and comfort. The mood was high, Robert was on the road to recovery, and they both left the room.

After the physicians removed his oral trach and left his room, I stayed, planning to spend the entire day in the ICU with him. What felt like a short time had passed; I entered his room and noticed a slight blue color on the right corner of his lower lip. It quickly progressed to turn both of his lips blue. I leaped from my chair, ran to the open door, where I saw the physician, and yelled, "Come quick, he is blue."

Chapter 6
Heaven: My First Visit

The moment I died, I left my body, and I found myself hovering above the frantic team of doctors and nurses who were valiantly trying to save my life. A very large male nurse was giving me CPR, and others were working on my neck trying to open my airway. I didn't feel any pain or panic. I was interested in watching what was happening but didn't realize the gravity of their efforts.

As I was watching what was going on inside my ICU room, I drifted to just outside my room and saw my Carol in the hallway, surrounded by nurses, her sobs and tears echoing in my mind. Then, just as quickly, I was no longer in the hospital but standing in the most beautiful place I had ever seen, Heaven.

I didn't go through a tunnel, nor did I see a bright light described by others who have had near-death experiences; I just arrived in Heaven. What I felt was like nothing I have ever felt in my life. Heaven is the most beautiful and welcoming experience I have ever seen or had, and it was beyond what I could ever imagine or describe completely.

I know that at times and places on earth, I and others have described a place or an experience we had as "This must be what Heaven is like" or "This is Heaven on earth." The moment I entered Heaven; I learned how inaccurate those comparisons are. There is no place on earth or experience on earth that compares to being in Heaven with Jesus.

The moment I entered Heaven I experienced and felt a Love and peace that could only come from Jesus. I had not met Jesus yet, but I could only imagine what it would be like to meet Jesus face to face. Neither did I know when or whether I was going to have that opportunity.

As I was looking around and trying to grasp the reality of where I was. I was awestruck by the breathtaking beauty. There was the most magnificent towering oak, magnolia, and a bounty of unidentifiable trees, all of them providing a canopy of shade. Scattered throughout were what I recognized as ornamental cherry blossoms, their vibrant pale pink blooms fluttering in the breeze. My home on Earth is surrounded by oak trees, but they are like dull twigs compared to the trees in Heaven. In Heaven, the color of the trees, leaves, and blossoms are the most vibrant and beautiful colors I have ever seen. Not only are they beautiful, but I felt connected to each one. Even the shade they provided flowed over me in a magnificent display of colors reflecting the color of the trees. It was as if I were being hugged by the shade, not just standing under the shade. Every corner of the flowers burst with color and the leaves are the greenest green imaginable. All the trees and flowers give off their own scent, and a sort of beautiful melodic hum or tone that harmonizes together, creating a very subtle and loving background noise that is peaceful, calming, and filled with Love. They are alive and part of Heaven, and it is as if they were welcoming me with their beauty and sound.

As I continued to look around, I saw a beautiful inner courtyard in the distance. I started to walk towards it, and the closer I got, I was amazed at the size and beauty of it. The courtyard can only be described as a breathtaking sanctuary of peace and divine splendor. I could see a bright glowing but soft light off in the distance of the massive courtyard. Also coming from what appeared to be that same light I saw a crystal-clear river of water flowing gently, its surface shimmering with light as it wound its way through the middle of the courtyard. Surrounding the river, the courtyard is lush with vibrant greenery. There are trees laden with fruit perfectly spaced throughout, filling the air with a sense of vitality and serenity. There are well-manicured hedges that line the golden pathways, interspersed with fragrant jasmine and lavender bushes, with their scents mingling in the air. The flowers burst from every corner with vibrant colors. Roses climb trellises, while tulips, daisies, and marigolds bloom in flowerbeds that add to the edging of the golden walkways. There are exotic flowers that I would describe as orchids and lilies that add an element of uniqueness and beauty, carefully arranged in pots near seating areas. The ground is covered with soft, thick, lush green grass.

The sky above is a luminous expanse of soft blues and gold, with fluffy, glowing clouds casting a divine ambiance over the scene. The courtyard is bathed in a light that engulfs everything and everyone with love, peace, and belonging.

As I entered the edges of the courtyard, the beauty was breathtaking. Then, I saw a familiar figure; my dad, who passed away in 2011. He was working in the inner courtyard, taking care of the trees, shrubs, and flowers, I tried to describe earlier, which are beyond any description of beauty. I felt a complete harmony with every flower, tree, and shrub. I knew at this point I had died and was in heaven.

My dad didn't appear or look like my dad as he did on earth at the time of his death at the age of 92. I remember my dad at the time of his death. I remember him as a frail man whose cancer had withered away the strong, healthy man I remembered from my youth. But now he looked like a healthy man of about 35 years old and everything around him was vibrant and alive in a way words can't capture. Trees, flowers, and shrubs hummed in harmony, and there was a warmth in the air that was both calming and exhilarating.

I walked over to my dad, and as I approached, I said, "dad?" When he responded, there was a unique softness to his voice, and he said in a familiar and sort of whimsical but kind way, "son, it looks like you did it this time". This was a familiar way my dad would greet me when I had done something out of the norm. I responded with, "I didn't do anything, I am in heaven, aren't I?" To which he lovingly replied, "Yes."

I looked around towards the bright, glowing but soft light in the far distance of the courtyard, only this time, I could see a silhouette of a man surrounded by the light. I asked my dad a question about who was in the far distant part of the garden standing in the glowing light. My dad responded with, "Who do you think it is?" I responded with a statement and question, "Is it Jesus?" His simple reply was no surprise: "Yes", he said. Then I asked how I could talk to Him. and My dad said, "First, you go over to Him and start by bending your right knee to the ground and then your left knee to the ground, and if there is to be a conversation, He will start it with you. You will experience something beyond anything you have ever experienced in life."

My dad and I talked a little more, and I looked around, trying to take in the beauty and vivid colors of all I could see.

The next thing I knew I was back in my room in the hospital, surrounded by doctors and nurses. I could breathe, but not through my mouth, but through my neck. It was a strange sensation, I tried to yell, "Hey, what are you doing?" but my mouth didn't work. I couldn't make a sound. At that time, the doctors had cut into my neck and inserted a tube to bypass the swollen airway in my throat. Little did I know that the tube they inserted into my neck to save my life would also be part of the reason that this would not be the last time I died and went to Heaven that day.

By this time, I had spent 15 minutes in heaven. I was going to experience death two more times very quickly that day.

What I experienced in those moments of clinical death was far beyond the realm of medical explanation. It was not just a dream or vision; it was an entrance into Heaven and a revelation of the eternity of joy and peace.

Chapter 7
"Carol, What Do You Want Us To Do?"

Once the doctor entered the room to address the fact that Robert had stopped breathing, I heard the overhead page "CODE BLUE ROOM 7 INTENSIVE CARE". That is Robert's Room!

"Heavenly Father, please place your hands on the people in Robert's room," was my first prayer.

Code Blue means that every available nurse and doctor on the shift is required to respond to a dire emergency.

"Hurry," "Don't wait," and "Send your best," were all thoughts rushing through my mind at the same time. How can this be? CPR for Robert?

Wait, he was just fine a few minutes ago; how can this be? The doctor said he was doing fine.

Wait, now he's getting CPR?

Before I could count to 10, there were literally a dozen doctors and nurses crowded into his very small ICU room, rushing in, shouting commands, shouting for equipment, devices, more room, more light. More! More! More!

"The tube won't go in!" "I can't get the airway to open".

Now I was sobbing, gripping my hands in prayer. "Please Jesus, please!" Tears were streaming down my cheeks and falling to the floor, gathering at my feet as the effort to remain calm slid from my eyes.

I think I must have gasped. I heard one nurse instruct another nurse to call the Chaplain to come to ICU room 7. The Chaplain? Has he died? Why do I need a Chaplain?

"Do you have any family that can come sit with you?" A voice crept into my sobs. "No, I am alone".

"Do you have any friends you can call?" "No, no one close enough to make it to the hospital now. I am all alone." Robert is my everything; who can I call who will understand my agony?

The Chaplain had arrived and was sitting facing me outside ICU room 7.

Fran, the Charge Nurse for that day, leaped from the doorway and rapidly asked me, "What do you want to be done?"

What do I want done? Do you mean he died, and you want me to decide between life and death? For Robert? For the love of my life?

I know I must have shouted my reply, trying desperately to be heard above the den of commotion going on inside Robert's room. "DO EVERYTHING!"

Fran re-entered the room, "His wife says to do everything! Keep going!"

Keep going? Do you mean the initial CPR didn't work?

The tenor of the staff in his room was like a tidal wave crashing into the shore, then receding to calm, then crashing into the shore, more shouting, more instructions, more equipment.

"It isn't working!"

"I need a larger tube!"

"Get me more gauze!"

"I need sterile coverages!"

"I can't stop the bleeding!"

"OK, he's back, he's back!"

So many different voices filled the room and the hallway.

"Thank you, Jesus, thank you for bringing Robert back to me. Thank you." I'm not sure but I think I was praying out loud.

"He's gone again!"

"Can you keep up the CPR, or do you want me to take over?"

"No, I'm fine" Faceless voices leaving Room 7, filling my mind.

More CPR? What happened was that he came back and now he needs more CPR.

"Get another Crash Cart; this one isn't enough!"

More? More Crash Carts, what could they need that they don't have?

"Dear God, I know you love him, and you know I love him too. Please God, send him to me, restore Robert to his full health. Keep your hands on the doctor's hands until he recovers".

"Do you want me to pray with you?" It was the Chaplain?" Of Course! The more prayers, the better; "Yes, please pray with me."

She began, "Dear Heavenly Father, please lay your hands on Carol and Robert. You know the love they share; you know everything about Robert and how much he loves Carol. You can see the work the doctors are doing to save his life, please allow Robert to live because of their efforts. Amen"

"He's Back!!" "He's Back!"

"Thank you, Jesus, thank you, Heavenly Father, for hearing my prayers. Thank you, Jesus for saving his life. You know I love him."

"He's coding again!" A nurse shouted. She continued, "Can you continue CPR, or do you need someone else to take over?" "No, I am fine, I am in the right place, and I am not tired"

"He's coding AGAIN! Bring another crash cart STAT!"

"Call the O.R., get the O.R. doctors up here. We can't establish the airway".

The loudspeaker blares "O.R. Doctors to ICU Room 7 STAT".

More doctors? What, why? Surely, he's going to be okay. Once the OR doctors get to the room, they can fix it, they can make it right.

Within what seemed like seconds, a team of scrubbed professionals marched up the hallway carrying all types of equipment, carts, tubes, bags, and a new gurney (later, I would realize it was to transport him to surgery). It reminded me of a movie when the rescuers arrived to "save the day".

The Operating Team established an airway. Relief swept over me. His airway was open, CPR worked, and he was alive.

What seemed like hours, was only a few minutes when the O.R. team took Robert from his room, covered in blood, and transported him on the gurney down the hall. I looked at him as he passed out of the room and down the hall. One nurse was using an Ambu bag (a portable mask with a squeeze device to keep oxygen moving into his lungs). He was covered with blood, his face swollen and silent, his left arm straight and gently responding to the movement of the gurney as they transported him rapidly to the operating room to secure the stoma and establish a method to attach a ventilator.

While I waited, I phoned my neighbors and asked them to please feed my dog, let him out, and make sure he had water. It was going to be a long night.

"Medical Cleaning Crew to ICU Room 7" announced the condition of Room 7. I managed to peer inside. The cleaning crew had a mess on their hands because the room looked like doctors were facing not only critical airway loss but massive blood loss.

It was well after midnight when Robert returned to Room 7. I couldn't leave until I knew that he survived the surgery. Exhausted, I visited with the nurses who were settling him into Room 7.

I was devastated and relieved at the same time. My emotions were on high alert, now confused and frightened. I waited until the surgery was over and he returned to the ICU.

It was after midnight when he returned to his room. A ventilator attached, IV bags. I counted 10, dripping life-saving medications into his system. I saw a tube in his shin and asked what was wrong with his leg.

"We needed to get medication into his system as fast as possible. That needle goes directly into the center of his shin bone, it's the fastest way to get the medication where it can do the most good."

"You should go home. He is asleep and doesn't know you are here." It was the night nurse. "Do you have someone who can come and get you?"

"No, I can make it. I want to come back tomorrow, and I will need my car to get here. I have a little dog at home who will be happy to see me." I found my way to the car, started it, and wiped away enough tears to find my way home.

I don't remember the 45-minute trip home, but before I knew it, I opened the garage door to walk into a lonely sight, my home, and a bedroom with an empty bed.

I barely slept because I was waiting for the phone to ring to tell me Robert passed away during the night. How could I leave him, what if he dies alone in the hospital? I spent the night tossing and turning, crying and praying.

The next morning, I waited for my neighbors to wake up before I left for the hospital. I filled them in on Robert's condition. Their first sentence was, "Don't worry about your dog; we will take care of everything; you just go to the hospital." And then, the supportive neighbors they are, added, "Call us and let us know how he is doing".

Chapter 8
Second Death and Heaven Again

I was back in my room in the ICU, surrounded by doctors and nurses. I could breathe, but not through my mouth, but through my neck. During the time I was in Heaven, the doctors had cut into my neck and inserted a tube to bypass the swollen airway in my throat.

It was, in what seemed to be a few minutes, my second death. I died the second time, and I was back in heaven. This time, when I died, I went to Heaven instantly without pausing above the doctors or nurses. Once again, I experienced the love and peace I had felt the first time. Just like the first time I went to Heaven, the beauty of Heaven, the smells in the air, and the feelings of being connected to everything and everyone was a welcoming familiarity of coming home.

Unlike the first time, this time I was standing at the edge of a beautiful field of tall grass that had the same beautiful trees scattered throughout. Looking to my left, in the far distance, I saw the inner courtyard and my dad was still there, but this time, my mom was there too.

She died in 1983, and she looked like she did when I was just a kid. I didn't approach them this time and no conversation took place. My mom didn't say anything to me but smiled the most beautiful smile I had ever seen her smile in my entire life.

I looked around, still in amazement at how beautiful everything was, how magnificent and bright the colors were, how warm and loving the light, sounds, and smells that filled the air were, and how peaceful and calm it was.

It was at this time I was treated to a surprise. Our pets that we love are in heaven!

Two horses and three dogs greeted me. The horses were Carol's; their names are Shakush and Nugget.

Shakush is a pure white Arabian who has the personality of a playful clown. When he was on earth, he would get into the arena with Carol, and together they would jump and play, more like a dog than a horse but much larger but just as gentle.

Carol raised and trained Shakush herself and was the only person who rode him. Carol was and still is an excellent horseperson and rider. She glides when riding, and it is a thing of beauty to watch. When Carol and Shakush were both younger, she would show him at horse shows, and they often finished in the top three. When Carol would ride him, he was always a perfect gentleman, and they would ride for hours in the arena and open fields. While running uphill on a trail he would buck, tossing his head in absolute joy. Regardless of the hill, the gait, or his mood, Carol could always brace herself for a joyful exuberant buck.

Nugget is a buckskin quarter horse and absolutely beautiful. She did not have the same personality as Shakush, but rather, she always acted very regal and gentle. Carol would ride Nugget, and on a rare occasion, she would share Nugget with me for a trail ride. Nugget was raised and trained by Carol just like Shakush. Both Shakush and Nugget were magnificent horses and were truly gifts and blessings from God.

Three dogs greeted me with our two horses. Two of the dogs that greeted me are named Fudge 1 and Fudge 2 because they are dark brown and sweet, just like Fudge. We named all of our dogs Fudge, so we don't get their name wrong when a new pet joins our family.

I did not recognize the third dog that approached me in Heaven with the others, I later learned the dog was named Annie and was Carol's dog before we met.

Fudge 1 was a rescue dog that was a sweet little dog that would run and play his game of catch me if you can. Of course, it was only when he decided to let us catch him that we were able to. Then he would cuddle up like the sweet dog he was. It was his way of playing. His special trick was the command, "What does a lion say?" he would imitate a lion in his own sweet sound.

Fudge 2 was used as a bait dog prior to our rescuing him. He wanted to be sweet and loving but had some prior issues because of his abuse before he became part of our family. There were times he would snap or have a flashback. It took a long time and a lot of love before he would trust us. He tried to overcome his past and did the best he could, and he turned out to be a sweet little boy.

He was unbelievably quick and would spring around like a bouncing ball. He still had flashbacks occasionally, stemming from when he was abused and treated so cruelly. When this happened, it was as if he recognized what he did and was sorry for snapping at us. Following his outburst, was when we got the most loving and cuddling from him. Our best efforts did not erase his abuse on earth. In heaven he's no longer like that. He is a happy puppy running and playing, with no signs of the remnants of his abuse.

The third dog's name was Annie. I didn't know the third dog's name until I was telling Carol about going to Heaven and our pets being there. It was when I was describing the dog I didn't recognize in heaven, that she told me it was her dog, Annie. Carol had Annie before I knew her. Mystery solved.

We currently have a dog, and of course, that is Fudge 3. He is a spitting image of Fudge 2, only sweeter.

When I was out of the hospital and was able to share with Carol my experiences in Heaven, she was beyond joyous, knowing the two horses she had and loved would be there, as well as our dogs. All of our animals were glad to see me and greeted me with love and kindness.

It was amazing seeing Shakush, Nugget, Fudge 1, Fudge 2, and Annie. We, unfortunately, had to put them to sleep because of old age, illnesses, or doggie dementia. They conveyed to me while visiting with them in Heaven, that they were aware of it and were thankful we did what we did to end their suffering.

In Heaven, you can communicate with your pets. I don't mean like we talk to other people, but in a unique way that God has made possible, so you and your pets know what you are thinking. So, if you have ever wondered what your pets are thinking, when you get to Heaven you will be able to share thoughts.

Our pets in Heaven continue to love us unconditionally and are extremely happy to be in Heaven. They will recognize you immediately upon your seeing them in Heaven.

I know now that the blessing of our pets that God gives us while here on earth, does not end when they die. God is caring for them until we enter Heaven, and we are reunited with them when we get there.

It is just one more blessing of many that you can look forward to; your pets are in Heaven, happy, healthy, and waiting to see you. You will have a more wonderful relationship with your pets in Heaven than you ever thought possible, and all eternity to enjoy them.

I was experiencing the joy of visiting with Shakush, Nugget, Fudge 1, Fudge2, and Annie, when the next thing I knew, I was back in my body and room 7 in the ICU, surrounded by doctors and nurses again.

I still could not breathe through my mouth, only through my neck. At the time, the doctors had cut into my neck and inserted a tube to bypass the swollen airway in my throat. That procedure caused a great deal of bleeding which unavoidably flowed freely into my lungs. Because I had a subsequent cardiac arrest, they performed a third round of CPR to get my heart beating again. This time, the bigger problem was that the amount of blood that had entered my lungs caused me to drown.

The doctors tried to stop the bleeding, and they were trying to get the blood out of my lungs; they tried gallantly because they knew that the oxygen they were pumping into me couldn't get into my bloodstream.

The doctors knew the urgency necessary to control the bleeding to prevent damaging the very fine membranes in the lungs that absorb the oxygen required to transmit oxygen into the bloodstream. When your heart pumps the blood with oxygen throughout your body to your brain, organs, muscles, etc., those vital organs use the vital oxygen to sustain life and all bodily functions.

With my blood clotting on the walls of my lungs, no oxygen was getting into my bloodstream. Every minute of oxygen deprivation was causing more damage to my brain, organs, and muscles in my body.

To put it plainly and simply, my brain and entire body were being destroyed by the lack of oxygen entering my bloodstream via the inside of my lungs. I was surpassing the point of any hope of survival.

My body was being kept alive by machines, but my vital organs continued to deteriorate because of oxygen deprivation. My brain, at this point, did not have the ability to tell my heart to beat or my lungs to work. None of my organs were working. Yet, the doctors continued to do all they could.

After I had flatlined this second time, the nurses went to Carol and asked her what she wanted them to do. The doctors knew that survival was not likely because of the time I had been without oxygen the first time I died. Also, they were aware of the brain damage I had suffered, and nothing could be done about it. Carol told them to do everything they could, and they followed her wishes.

As they continued diligently working on me and trying to clear my lungs from blood and get oxygen into my bloodstream, I died the third time. The lack of oxygen and stress was too great for my weakening body, and I subsequently suffered a third cardiac arrest.

Like the second time I died, I was immediately standing in Heaven. Only this time, I was standing in the inner courtyard. I didn't know it yet, but this time was going to be much longer. The first time, I was in Heaven for 15 minutes, and the second time, I was in Heaven for

17 minutes. This time was my third time, and it was going to last for 43 hours and 28 minutes and be much more revealing. I was going to see and meet Jesus.

Chapter 9
Third Death And Heaven Again

As they continued working on me and trying to clear my lungs from the blood and get oxygen into my bloodstream, I died the third time. The lack of oxygen and stress was too great for my weakening body, and I subsequently suffered a third cardiac arrest. This involved a third round of CPR.

Once again, I was immediately standing in Heaven for the third time. Only this time, I was standing in the inner courtyard.

I was asking myself, "How is this possible? Is this really happening?" The first time, I was in Heaven for 15 minutes and saw my dad, the second time, I was in Heaven for 17 minutes and learned our pets are in Heaven, and I was able to visit with them. Both of those times were a miracle and a blessing in themselves.

Now I was standing in Heaven, for the third time. But unlike the other two times, I found myself in the inner courtyard, and although I didn't know it yet, I was going to be in Heaven this time for 43 hours and 28 minutes.

I was about to have my questions answered and so much more in a way that I can only describe it as the greatest blessing I have ever experienced.
I was going to meet Jesus!

As I stood in the inner courtyard looking around, I was trying to grasp the reality of where I was, and the breathtaking beauty of it. The magnificent towering oaks, the bounty of trees, and the now familiar, comforting hum and canopy of shade flowed over me like a welcoming hug. The scent of cherry blossoms and vibrant colors filled the air. Once again, I felt connected to everything.

As I took in the beauty of Heaven, I saw Jesus standing in the distance, and I began walking toward Him. The light around Him is radiant, not blinding but comforting, a warmth that filled every corner of my soul. As I approached Jesus, I was immediately overwhelmed by being in His presence and fell to the ground. His love radiated outward and completely filled and surrounded me. I could do nothing but weep tears of love, joy, gratitude, and humility. I realized that I was in the presence of my Lord and Savior, and His love was unlike anything I had ever experienced. It filled every part of me, a love that was unconditional, boundless, and unending.

Jesus stood and came to me; He stretched out His hand and said, "Everything will be alright; take My hand, stand and walk with Me."

I would like to be able to describe what I was feeling at that moment. However, there are no words outside of heaven that could ever describe the love and comfort that can only come from being in His presence. This is Jesus, my Lord and Savior, the Creator and

Sustainer of the Universe, who is going to hold my hand and walk with me in Heaven. I can only tell you to do your best to imagine how you would feel or react. It is overwhelming, humbling, and feeling loved beyond anything you or I could imagine.

Jesus stretched His hand out and took mine in His; He helped me up and literally wiped away my tears. He told me that He had many things to show me and much to talk about and teach me. His voice was full of compassion and understanding. He knew everything about me, my life, my love for Carol, the pain I had experienced in dying, and the love I was feeling in Heaven.

As Jesus took my hand in His, the warmth that spread through me was indescribable. It was a feeling of being loved, belonging, and of being home. When I was able to stand with Jesus' help, I looked into His eyes; the love and caring that flowed from His eyes filled me with the greatest love I have ever felt.

Jesus' eyes can only be described as pure love and truth. When Jesus spoke, I knew that whatever He said was absolute truth conveyed from love. I knew that everything was going to be alright. I also knew I was about to be shown around Heaven by Jesus.

As Jesus and I started out walking on roads and paths made of gold so pure they were almost translucent, He explained how and why this was happening to me. Knowing that everything Jesus says is the truth, I knew that whatever He talked to me about, taught me, or showed me while walking with Him was going to be an amazing experience and blessing.

Jesus and I walked hand in hand, and He showed me where I would live in Heaven: a home of incredible beauty, with walls made of glowing, precious materials, similar to a beautiful stained glass window that radiates rainbows of light, a pasture without fences, and a flowing stream of the clearest water I have ever seen. There are groves of towering trees, beautiful flowers, and plush green grass. In the pasture, Carol's horses were playing and running freely. Our dogs were also jumping and playing with our horses.

Jesus and I stood at the edge of the pasture watching Shakush, Nugget, and my dogs playing. Then Shakush, Nugget, and our 3 dogs ran to where Jesus and I were standing to greet us. It was the most loving, coolest, and amazing thing I had ever experienced. I was standing in Heaven, where I would live, with Jesus, and He was petting our horses, and they were enjoying every second of it.

Heaven is truly alive with God's love and is a place where all things are connected by His Love and light.

Jesus continued to walk with me and showed me around Heaven. He explained to me that what I was seeing was Heaven, but this would not be where all believers in Him would spend all of eternity.

Immediately, my thoughts went to what Jesus was saying. What He said was contrary to everything I thought about Heaven. I believed that if I were a true believer in Christ, I would be forgiven and would spend all of eternity in Heaven with Jesus.

Before I could gasp at this new revelation, Jesus continued to share why that was true. He told me that He had explained throughout the Old and New Testament that true believers will spend all eternity in Heaven with Him. But it will be the New Heavens and New Earth, which will then be Heaven.

Jesus told me that one day in the future, He would return to the present Earth, and all that have believed and put their faith and trust in Him, and the "dead in Christ" will meet Him in the air. Jesus said when that happens, He will destroy all of His enemies.

Jesus explained that the present earth and all that is in it are under the same curse of sin that affects all mankind. He said He would make everything new, including the Earth and Heavens and all that ever existed.

He would sanctify and redeem the very soil of the Earth of today, to enable our redeemed and sanctified bodies to live upon it.

He said the New City of Jerusalem would go down from the current Heaven and set upon the new Earth, making it the New Heaven and New Earth. He would then reside on the New Earth in the New City of Jerusalem and be amongst and with His children for all of Eternity.

As Jesus and I continued to walk, He shared many more things with me in addition to what the New Heaven and the New Earth would be like. I am going to share what Jesus shared with me, but first, I want to explain How and why Jesus blessed me with the miracle of life after my dying three times.

Chapter 10
My Final Conversation With Jesus

Jesus and I arrived back at the inner courtyard and sat on a bench under the canopy of towering trees with fragrant flowers on the edge of the River of Life. We were about to have a conversation about whether I would be staying in Heaven or returning to my life on Earth.

As I sat with my Lord and Savior, I felt more loved and welcomed than I ever felt in my life. I felt like I belonged, and I was home.

Jesus started the conversation. He said, "Before our walk, you told Me that you were concerned about Carol because of how your death was affecting her. You asked Me if you could go back and comfort and take care of her. I heard you but did not answer then because I had much to share with you. I needed to know that if you were allowed to go back it would be for the right reasons. Your love in your heart would make the decision and would have to be made without any ulterior motives and without any selfish reasons whatsoever."

Jesus continued, "I know your desire to return is from the love you have for Carol, and it was truly to comfort and continue to love her. This is the third time you have died and come here. As a result of your death, your body has suffered much damage. If I were to just send you back and allow the doctors to continue medical treatment and life support, the death of your brain cells and deterioration of your organs and body parts would make it impossible for you to have a normal life. You would be confined within yourself and be unable to care for yourself or comfort Carol.-Therefore, you would be staying in Heaven."

Jesus continued, "I could and would send you back with some caveats. Let Me explain, if you choose to have Me send you back, I will give you a renewed brain, organs, and body parts that will allow you to function as if you never died. It will enable you to comfort and care for Carol. You will have a complete memory of your life, including what I shared and taught you while in Heaven."

Jesus then told me what He would require me to do, "You will worship Me in Truth and Spirit, and you will do as I command you."

"In doing so you will share how and why you were given life again."

"You will share with anybody that I put in your path and will entertain any questions about what I shared and taught you from anybody who asks."

Jesus continued, "If you go back, you will endure all the pain and discomfort from the moment you enter your body until you heal. This includes all procedures and surgeries the doctors perform on you. You will feel all of this as though you had no anesthesia."

Jesus went on to explain, "If you survive this pain, then I will allow the doctors to resuscitate you and continue the medical treatments you will need.".

Jesus instructed me, "Now you must make a choice."
"The choice to stay in Heaven with Me, and as I shared, you will not be able to look down on Carol, and you will not know anything that she is going through. You will not be able to comfort her; you will not have any memory of her until she arrives in Heaven."

"Or you may choose to go back and accept that you're going back with all the caveats I disclosed to you. You will worship Me in truth and spirit, and you will do as I command you."

Jesus told me that whatever I chose, I would be all right, but it would have to be a pure, unselfish decision on my part.

I looked at Jesus and told Him my choice. I told Him I wanted to go back and that it would be an honor and blessing to share all that I learned while with You in Heaven.

I know Jesus searched my heart, and I must have had the right motives in my heart, because I was sitting in Heaven with Jesus one moment, and the next moment, I was back in the ICU.

Chapter 11
Back To The ICU For The 3rd Time.

Jesus did exactly what He told me He would do. Instantly, I was back in my body in the ICU. Jesus sent me back and gave me a fully functioning brain with no damage or disability, complete with all memories and the ability to control my bodily functions and process pain.

My body and organs would be regenerated and become fully functioning from the commands and intact workings of my fully functioning brain and the medical care that I would receive from the physicians and medical staff while in the hospital.

I also would feel all the pain and suffering from when I entered my body until I was discharged.

Jesus sent me back into my body that was in a medically induced coma. I was being given a continuous IV of fentanyl PF so I would not feel pain, and a continuous IV of propofol for anesthesia to keep me in the medically induced coma. By all medical reasoning and as far as the doctors knew, I would not be aware of anything, and I would not feel any pain.

Facility-Administered Medications noted in the medical record:

Medication	Route	Frequency	Last Rate
• fentanyl PF	Continuous IV Infusion	CONTINUOUS	25 mcg/hr (05/18/24 0844)

•*propofol*	*Continuous* *IV Infusion*	*CONTINUOUS40* *mcg/kg/min* *(05/18/24* *0728)*

However, the physicians, medical staff, and Carol were not aware that I had gone to Heaven three times and that Jesus was in control, not them. I knew I was going to live and have a full life serving Jesus; they did not.

They also did not have any idea that my brain was fully functioning, that I was aware of everything that was taking place, and that I would feel all the pain even though I was sedated and should not feel a thing.

The moment Jesus returned me to my body, the discomfort and pain began. I had tubes and IVs inserted in my arms and legs. I was connected to life support machines that were controlling my body functions to keep me alive.

The life support machines, tubes, and IVs did not cause much pain, but they certainly caused a great deal of discomfort. I was unable to talk or move any part of my body.

The pain that I felt was excruciating. I felt every time they poked and prodded me. I had four broken ribs which were painful enough. But every two hours they would come into my room and roll me over to protect my skin from breaking down. When they would roll me over it felt like I was being stabbed by a sharp knife emanating from my broken ribs. They were only doing what was necessary and they had no idea I was feeling any pain. I wanted to cry out in pain for them to stop. Because of the medically induced coma, I was in, I couldn't because I was unable to move or talk. I could only endure and wait for them to come back in two more hours.

I felt every surgical procedure they performed: the tracheostomy, and the incision on the mass on my neck. I felt every time they gave me a shot every evening in my stomach to reduce the risk of blood clots.

I continued to endure the pain and discomfort including when they took me back to surgery to remove additional blood clots in my lungs.

During this procedure, I was begging them to stop because of the pain. But I was the only one that could hear it. I was not able to move or make a sound. The Surgeons had no idea that I could feel anything, so they continued.

As far as the physicians knew my brain was not functioning because of brain cells that had died due to oxygen deprivation. I was showing no signs of improvement.

I did not wake up until May 31st, and Carol was at my bedside every day that I was in the hospital. She was my biggest advocate and never gave up hope. When the doctors would tell her there was no hope, she told them to do more and continued praying.

Carol learned everything there was to learn about how to understand the information the machines delivered while keeping me alive.

Carol did everything possible to make me comfortable and help me recover fully.

Chapter 12
After My Discharge From The Hospital

The day I was discharged from the hospital on June 19th, 2024, Carol was there to take me home.

After my discharge, when I required physical therapy, Carol would drive me to and from the therapy.

She cared for my every need including helping me take showers until I was able to do so on my own.

I had to build up strength to be able to stand and learn to walk on my own. Carol would take me and my walker to big department stores that were air conditioned where we would walk the aisles together. They must have wondered why this old guy on a walker never bought anything, so Carol made sure we went to different stores, so they didn't think we were up to anything.

I was able to gain strength, and I can walk on my own with no sign of anything ever being wrong. I am able to play golf again and can do everything I did before.

The love and support that Carol gave me could not be measured. She truly is my personal angel and the love of my life.

Thank you Carol.

I love you beyond words could ever express and I want you to always remember I am yours.

Chapter 13
Thank You Jesus

Jesus sent me back and let me live after dying three times. He kept His Word by the miracle He blessed me with. I have a fully functioning brain with complete memories; my heart and all the organs in my body are perfect and functioning. Just as Jesus told me, "It is as if I had never died, except I did, I went to Heaven, and Jesus gave me another life."

I thank Jesus for this blessed life every day. I am so appreciative that He allowed me to comfort and love Carol.

Just like before my death, I play golf, but I enjoy it so much more. I enjoy everything more because I fully realize that in our lives, everything we have and enjoy is a miracle and a blessing from Jesus.

Jesus restored my body and gave me life after I died, it is Jesus who lives in and through me, and I look forward to the blessing of serving Him. I count it as a blessing for every person I meet to share the miracle Jesus blessed me with and spread the hope and understanding that Jesus is alive, and those who have faith and trust in Him will one day be in Heaven with Him.

Thank you Jesus, for my miracle, my new life, and Carol, the love of my life.

Chapter 14
Carol's Point Of View; Monday, May 20, 2024

After a sleepless night, I got out of bed early, and as I usually do, my dog Fudge got up when I did and was waiting for me to open his crate. When I opened his crate, he bounded out looking for Robert for the start of his morning rituals.

I usually get up first, make the coffee, and then feed Fudge. He waited patiently to go outside, and then inside for his usual morning meal. He has a cute habit of hopping on his front feet for his meal. This cute habit of his was a welcome ritual of my usual day. I know it is a small ritual, but at the time, it was the first "normal" part of my day.

My neighbors had fed Fudge the night before and filled his water dish. I fed him, and his next usual routine was to greet Robert after he got out of bed. I left the bedroom door open since I did not need to worry about disturbing Robert's sleep.

Fudge sauntered into the bedroom and put his front paws on Robert's side of the bed. Since he could not see him or smell him, he began his search through the house. First the couch. Then the office, then the bathroom, smelling the floor for Robert's scent. Not finding Robert, he came to my feet, sat down, looked up at me, and gave me his cute whine, "Where's Robert?"

I got into the shower in hopes the bags below my eyes would miraculously deflate so I looked like I rested. I did what I could with my makeup to look a little bit presentable.

At 7:00 my phone rang.

"How's Robert?" asked Deby, my neighbor who took care of my dog the previous day.

"I have not called the hospital yet. They did not call during the night, so I suspect he has not changed. I am going to go to the hospital and see him in a few minutes." I gave her a gloomy response.

"Well, call us if you want us to take care of Fudge for you." They are great neighbors, and I am thankful I can count on them.

My 45-minute drive to the hospital was a blur. People going about their routine drive to work or school. My mind was on how Robert did during the night. I slept with the phone next to my bed with instructions to the nurse to call me if there were any changes. I tried to convince myself that no news is good news.

Exiting the elevator, it is a sharp left, then another sharp left to the electronic doors to enter the ICU. Immediately, in the front of the ICU entrance are the rules: No flowers, no children under the age of 14, and no photos were just a few of the obvious rules that ask for respect and quiet behavior.

I could look directly into room 7 and see Robert lying on his left side, bed propped up to the correct angle to prevent aspiration.

I walked to his room, he was sleeping, heavily sedated. The nurse walked into the room and introduced herself, she reported he rested well throughout the night. I suggested he may be still under the influence of the anesthesia from the night before, but she said the anesthesia had worn off, and he was sedated to keep him from attempting to remove his ventilator tubing or IV lines.

Approaching him, I could feel tears well up in my eyes and silently flow onto my cheeks. I knew he was desperately ill, clinging to life. Too soon to know the outcome. After what he had suffered the day before, I knew there was a chance he would have permanent brain damage with resulting disabilities.

I did not want to dwell on the possibility of a life of disabilities, so I stopped the negative thoughts by praying. I asked God to please give me the strength to be thankful for the life in front of us, to be with the doctors and nurses who hold his well-being in their hands.

I spent the day sitting by his bed, hoping for improvements in his oxygen saturation, white count, or any good news.

During the morning rounds, the same physician who cared for Robert in the Emergency Room came into Robert's room and addressed me.

"He has a lot of blood clots in his lungs. I want to take him to the operating room and conduct a bronchoscopy to remove as many clots as I can. Will you sign the consent?"

"Yes, of course," I replied. "Please do everything you can." I will wait until you finish so you can let me know what you find.

"It will be later this evening; I have a full day ahead of me; I can have the nurses fill you in later."

The Bronchoscopy started at 5:50 that night.

From the Medical Record:

> **H&P Update Pre-Procedure** - *This patient has been examined and there have been NO changes in the patient's medical status. The necessity of the procedure or care is still present. The H&P is current.*
>
> **Procedure** - *Bronchoscopy with therapeutic aspiration of secretions and bronchoalveolar lavage.*
>
> **Description of procedure** - *After a time out was performed, adequate local anesthesia and IV sedation was given. The fiberoptic bronchoscope was passed via the tracheostomy and the trachea was entered. The carina was sharp. The left and right mainstem bronchi were visualized. A full tracheo-bronchial tree survey was performed. Specimens were obtained without complication. The bronchoscope was subsequently removed. The patient tolerated the procedure well.*

Findings -

Thick endobronchial secretions observed throughout all the airways.

Thick mucus plugs observed occluding the distal aspect of the right bronchus intermedius

Mucus plug appeared to be mixed with blood clot.

This was aspirated and the distal airways were visualized.

Bronchial lavage was performed of the right lower lobe.

I stayed in the ICU until Robert returned to room 7. The nurses gave me a little information about the procedure, stating the physician would fill me in tomorrow.

It was extremely late when I phoned Deby. I gave her what little information I had and let her know Robert was heavily sedated and as stable as he could be for someone who endured what he had gone through.

Deby said, "We let Fudge out around 2:00. Kevin took him out to the backyard and threw the ball for a while. I do not know who had the most fun, Kevin or Fudge."

I told Deby, "Knowing Fudge, he played until his tongue hung out, then slept the rest of the day. I appreciate your help with Fudge, it means a lot to me."

I am sure I sounded exhausted, but Deby didn't acknowledge my angst. Instead, she said very kindly, "You don't need to worry about Fudge, we will take care of him, and you can take care of yourself."

Before I hung up, I let her know I would call her tomorrow and welcomed her offer to let Fudge out the next day.

I slept very little that night. I kept the phone next to my bed. I had nagging fears that Robert would pass away, alone in Room 7.

Chapter 15
Tuesday, May 21, 2024
Carol's Point Of View

Each time I woke up, I looked at the clock, counting the minutes until I could get up, shower, and get to the hospital to meet with the physician for an explanation of what occurred during the night and what was planned to take place that day.

This morning was the same routine for me and Fudge. He could not find Robert anywhere in the house, no matter how hard he searched.

I gave him his breakfast and left for the hospital around 8:00. I did not want to get there before the nurses changed shifts at 7:00; that way, I wouldn't be in the way while the nurses exchanged vital information. I knew rounds started at 9:00 and I made certain to be there to hear about his care planning.

It was Tuesday morning, and traffic was the predictable commuting traffic. I had to force myself to concentrate and stay focused on the thought of safety; I couldn't risk being in an accident and leaving Robert on his own.

I arrived at the ICU and found Robert sleeping soundly. His wrists were restrained and attached to the bed. The nurse said it was common for people recently intubated to prevent them from attempting to remove the ventilator equipment.

In the hospital, rounds begin at 9:00. Completing rounds is a daily occurrence, with the direct care team going from patient to patient, describing the prior 24 hours, and coming to an agreement for care planning.

I asked the nurse to please inquire whether I could remove the wrist restraints while I was in attendance. He was heavily sedated, and motionless, so I knew he would not be capable of moving his arms, or any other body part for that matter.

She spoke to the team, and the answer was, "Yes, the wrist restraints may be removed permanently." I cried.

I also asked if the physicians could lance the infection mass on his neck in the hopes the antibiotics had more of a chance to take care of less infected areas and hopefully heal that area faster.

I cried every day, sometimes several crying episodes. The first days were all tears of fear, sadness, and hopelessness. From my experience of working with patients who suffered strokes, head injuries, and brain damage, I was fully aware of the possibility that I had lost Robert, or at least the Robert he was before. I was concerned with him suffering life-altering brain damage.

After rounds, the physician who performed the bronchoscopy the previous evening came to Room 7 to meet with me. He explained the procedure he performed and let me know he removed several large clots in his lungs and wanted to remove more, but Robert wasn't tolerating the procedure well enough for him to complete as much as he wanted. But he went on to say, what he removed should make a significant difference in his recovery. More tears and those tears were for the gratitude of removing dangerous blood clots.

The nurse came into his room after the physician left and shared with me the reputation of this specific physician. It seems we were blessed with one of the top (if not the top) pulmonologists in the country. She stated he is the most aggressive pulmonologist for implementing procedures other pulmonologists elect not to perform. She showered praises on this particular physician and assured me Robert was in excellent hands. This time I cried with relief that Jesus sent the best doctor to care for Robert.

I did a lot of crying during Robert's stay. I am admitting something here, I used the hospital's tiny little boxes of tissues. When they were empty, I would go to the nurse with an empty box and state, "Please put this on Robert's bill, I am going to rack up some more charges." Comedy can be a stress reliever for me.

I left for home around 6:30 that evening, giving the rush hour traffic some time to diminish a little. I decided my drive home was a perfect time to make calls to the important people in our lives: his brother, daughter, and several friends. My only connection to people was a phone call since my days were spent in the hospital where visitors are limited.

Deby and her husband, Kevin, live across the street from us. There are no better neighbors than Deby and Kevin. We have lived in our current home for four years. Every day of those four years has been the best four years in terms of neighbors than anywhere else we have lived. Before I could even think of something I might need, Deby and Kevin had already thought of it and taken care of it.

Chapter 16
Wednesday, May 22, 2024
Carol's Point of View

I arrived at the hospital at around 9:00 just as rounds were beginning. The nurse told me that since the nurse was conveying my questions, I had been invited to join rounds for Robert. I was able to engage the entire care team with my questions and clarify their answers if I didn't understand.

It is a delicate dance to ask the right questions without arguing my point of view while attempting to understand the treatments and medications prescribed.

A new CT was conducted, and the results of a new CT scan showed an additional abscess forming on the left side of Robert's neck. It looks like new issues are starting and the antibiotics are not preventing his infection from worsening. It seems new antibiotics would be necessary.

Late the evening of May 22nd, the ENT (Ear, Nose, and Throat) physician took Robert to the operating room to lance the infection on the left side of Robert's neck. It was the infection that was causing the airway to become blocked. Following the surgery, the physician called me at home to let me know the surgery went well and all the infection was removed. The surgery notes indicate both areas of infection were drained and irrigated. The surgeon placed a drain to ensure all the infection left the body and didn't stay inside the wound.

Chapter 17
Thursday, May 23, 2024
Robert Squeezed My Fingers!
Carol's Point of View

White blood cell count was improving; following the surgery, the infection was removed, another slight improvement.

Every day when I arrived, I noticed his hands were particularly swollen, his fingers were individually swollen, as well as the backs of his hands and palms. I asked if I could massage his hands back toward his forearms to relieve the swelling. The answer was "of course." So, I spent several minutes, several times a day massaging his hands. I purchased antibiotic hand cream to add moisture to his hands. I am not sure he was aware of my efforts to reduce the swelling, but just in case, I was determined to do it every day.

I sat beside the bed, as usual, and turned on the TV in his room as a distraction. I spent most days massaging his hands to move the edema back into his arm and reduce the puffiness. I had just finished Robert's hand massage and was merely holding his hand, using his curled fingers, and placing my two fingers inside his bent hand.

Wait! Did he just squeeze my fingers? What? Did I imagine it? I squeezed back. No, I did not imagine it; he did it again! I stretched for a third squeeze, but it did not happen. Yes, you guessed it, I cried.

Wiping away tears I stepped out to tell his nurse. "He squeezed my hand! Twice!" She stood up and said, "He did that to me this morning, but I was afraid it was just a reflex, so I didn't mention it to you."

"Nope, I am certain he did it twice, once on his own and once after I returned his squeeze." More tears and more tissues charged to Robert's hospital bill.

At this time, Robert's eyes remained open, unable to close them. His pupils remained pinpoint and slightly reactive to light. The nurses applied ointment, and eye drops to keep his eyes moist. It was difficult to watch so I would close his eyelids to attempt to make his eyes more comfortable and make him look like he was sleeping. When his eyes were open, it reminded me that he could not control his eyelids, and I felt like if I could help him move even that small body part, somewhere his brain would take over that part. I would wipe the excess ointment and drops from his face after treatment, wash his face, and give him a kiss on the forehead.

By now the nurses were used to seeing me in the room all day and gave me permission to retrieve my own clean washcloths from the linen cart. I felt useful.

At this point, I was worried about extensive brain damage. None of the hospital professionals had discussed brain MRI findings conducted on May 20th, so I was unaware of his original MRI. The physician's note on this day stated:

Wife states that she does not want to continue to cause suffering and if the MRI shows anoxic injury she will want to discuss with palliative.

Palliative care focuses on improving the quality of life for people with serious illnesses and their care partners. Once the team decided to provide palliative care, their focus was more on comfort measures, and extra support for me to cope with Robert's condition.

Earlier in the day, the ICU manager had initiated a conversation with me regarding Robert's condition and probable outcomes. I felt him edging toward a discussion of life support, and whether it was in Robert's best interest to end life support.

Before he could finish, I offered him information about our Living Will. I discussed with him my career involvement with individuals who suffered anoxia, (oxygen deprivation). I further explained that we have Living Wills for each other, and our living will state that we elect to be kept alive for 14 days on a ventilator before deciding whether to continue life support. He honored Robert's wishes.

Later that day, his pulmonologist met with me in his room. I expressed to him that earlier Rober had squeezed my fingers. I also told him that I thought Robert might have suffered a stroke, likely in his brain stem since his eyes were so unreactive. He looked at me, taking a moment to think about what I had just told him. He then told me he was not a neurologist, but he didn't think the brain had suffered a stroke.

"Let's do this," he started. "I will reduce his sedation medication to a level where he might respond to a simple instruction. I will come back in two hours, and we shall see."

Okay, I looked at the time on my phone. It was the longest two hours of my life. Waiting and waiting, pacing, checking my phone for e-mails, I was too nervous to sit still.

Finally, two hours passed, and his pulmonologist was on time, right to the dot. He lowered Robert's bed to enable himself to talk directly into Robert's left ear. "I am your doctor; I want you to raise both of your arms," he shouted to make sure he could hear through the fog of pain medication and sedation.

Robert raised both arms together, straight up to the ceiling without hesitation. The physician was startled at Robert's response and inadvertently shoved the stool he was sitting on back, out of surprise.

He returned quickly and continued. "Wiggle your toes." Robert immediately wiggled his toes on both feet at the same time, at the same pace.

"Look at me." Robert immediately turned his head.

"Blink your eyes." Robert blinked his eyes once or twice.

"Blink them really fast." Robert blinked both eyes rapidly and equally.

"He has not had a stroke. I am not exactly sure what exactly is going on, but to make sure, I will order a follow-up MRI of his brain.

The tears flowed and flowed and flowed. I used another box of tissues, and I was happy to keep using up his endless supply.

Once I overcame my joy, I slowly realized a new challenge: could he be weaned from the ventilator? Our Living Will indicates if he were to be confined to bed for the rest of his life, I was instructed to end life support. I cried again.

I called Deby. "He has not had a stroke! The doctor just left, and he has not had a stroke".

"That's great news, what did the doctor say?" I told her of the instructions and the pending MRI. She was as happy as I was.

I drove up to my house that afternoon, and my lawn had been mowed. When Robert got sick, he was planning to mow that day, the grass was teetering on the edge of becoming a forest. Kevin had mowed my yard, side yard, and back yard…the entire acre. I have great neighbors; how does one thank a neighbor who effortlessly takes over your responsibilities?

Chapter 18
Friday, May 24, 2024
MRI Results
Carol's Point of View

Today is Robert's birthday. I had some major changes to celebrate. First, he didn't suffer a stroke. Next, he is still fighting, and finally, I know God hears my prayers.

The MRI results should be back today, and I couldn't wait. I asked the nurse to please read his chart and let me know what the MRI results showed. Nurses are not supposed to share test results with family members or patients.

"Let me take a look; the results may not be back yet; it was pretty late when he went down for the MRI, and even if I have the results, we aren't supposed to reveal them to the family; that is the physician's role."

"Okay, I will be patient, I know how important it is for a nurse to not misinterpret results and deliver news that may be incomplete or inaccurate."

"Well," she said. "The results are in. I'm not saying anything, but if I were you, I would be very optimistic."

Optimistic? I cannot believe it. I took that to mean it was going to be good news. I am ready to hear the results. Hopefully, this will be another cause to celebrate his birthday.

Rounds started and 9:00, and the team needed to address the neighboring patients, starting with room number 1. In what seemed like hours, the team eventually got to room 7. They covered the usual overnight labs, temperature, ventilator settings, and then, finally, the MRI results: Normal brain activity, no signs of anoxia or stroke.

Wait…say that again! Did I hear it right? No, he can follow single-step commands; his brain is free from injury. How can this be? I have hope. Yes, I cried again.

I was walking around the room, a bit bored, when I looked out the window as I have done several times a day, I noticed a tiny glass duck, about the size of my pinky finger, sitting on the windowsill. It was positioned to face the room. A tiny little glass duck, yellow with an orange bill. I had not noticed it before, but there it was. Just sitting there. I do not know how it got there, or who put it in Robert's room, but it was a comfort to me for some odd reason. After that, every time I came into his room, I looked for that tiny glass duck. It may have been there the whole time, and I had not noticed, but I noticed that day, and every day after that for his entire stay. My little spark of joy, a little glass duck.

That afternoon a hospital volunteer approached Robert's room with a birthday balloon on a stick, along with a birthday card from the hospital. Hmmm, a birthday card for a man who is fighting to stay alive. Yes, I cried. I cried for him unable to know it was his birthday, unable to know I was kissing his cheek, unable to know I was massaging his hands. Unable to hear me sing Happy Birthday (well, maybe missing my singing was his gift this year).

On this day, I took particular notice of the job the Respiratory Therapists were doing each time they treated Robert. Before now, I silently watched them go about their very specific care, suctioning, and adjusting nobs in the ventilator. Today, for the first time, I asked them to explain the important numbers they needed to determine if he was becoming less dependent on the ventilator.

I learned three important settings: PEEP Score, Oxygen concentration, and Oxygen saturation.

PEEP: Positive End Expiratory Pressure. It refers to the pressure that is always present in the lungs. It prevents the Alveolar collapse at the end of exhalation. In Robert's case, the Alveola had been compromised when the blood entered his lungs and formed clots. Normal PEEP in healthy lungs is 5-8; Robert's PEEP score was 16. A PEEP score is the highest level at which maximum expiratory pressure is reached. PEEP scores above 12 have a 26% greater mortality rate.

The Respiratory Therapists stated that Physical Therapists will not work with patients until the PEEP score is 7 or lower. I knew I could do something about that!

Oxygen Concentration: This setting is adjusted to between .21 (room air) to 100% oxygen, meaning that the patient requires all the oxygen to be delivered by the ventilator. At the beginning, and during the nights, Robert's setting was 100%.

Oxygen Saturation: Oxygen saturation is measured by a small device, typically on a finger; most of us have used that device when we go to our doctor for a check-up or if we are being cared for in the emergency room. In Robert's case, it was clipped to his earlobe. Oxygen saturation measures the amount of oxygen in the blood cells. Normally it is measured while the patient is breathing without the support of supplemental oxygen. Physicians and Respiratory Therapists are interested in the amount of oxygen that is bound to hemoglobin. For a normal person who does not need oxygen support, normal saturation is between 95% and 100%.

The goal for Robert was to never let it fall below 80%. The Respiratory Therapist shared that if it falls below 80%, an alarm sounds, and the oxygen saturation percentage has to be increased.

In Robert's case, the Respiratory Therapists adjust the oxygen and PEEP administration according to his oxygen saturation. I became a warrior watching the PEEP and Oxygen data.

Respiratory Therapists are the most remarkable team members to care for Robert. Regardless of the alarm sounds, or the painful necessary coughing stimulated by suctioning, Respiratory Therapists are unshakable.

Hour by hour, minute by minute, I would watch his screens to see if his saturation levels maintained a level above 80%, if the Respiratory Therapists felt he could manage with less oxygen, and if he could start to breathe on his own.

There were several times that the alarm would sound indicating he stopped breathing. It took a couple of times before I realized it was common for the oximeter attached to his ear to fall off. It was not long before I felt like I was able to solve a problem myself without interrupting the nurse who was busy helping other patients.

There were times of joy and times of discouragement. And the support of those professionals cannot be understated.

Chapter 19
Saturday, May 25, 2024
Carol's Point of View

At the suggestion of a friend of mine, I brought a book to read to Robert. She suggested that simply talking to him was good, but not enough. She believed that auditory brain stimulation may improve his well-being as well as stimulate portions of his brain. She went on to suggest if he could not watch TV, at least find a way to play music throughout the day. She thought the music might be a welcome change from the talking and reading.

Hearing my voice, even if he couldn't comprehend what I was saying, was worth a try; a familiar voice among clinical voices may make a difference. Even if it was only a slight stimulation, I thought it was worth a try. I brought a book by his favorite author, David Baldacci. I pulled up a chair and read Chapter 1. As lunchtime rolled around, I took a break and told him we could resume the book after I had a sandwich.

I left the room and found a quiet place for a quick bite. I came back and started to read again. Up until now, he did not make any motions as recognition that he could hear me, much less understand what I was saying. I asked him if he wanted to listen to Chapter 2. He gave me a decided NO movement with his head. Well, I guess that was that! I asked him if it was my reading or the subject matter…he didn't answer.

Chapter 20
Sunday, May 26, 2024
Carol's Point of View

The good news, he was able to tolerate a PEEP setting of 14, down from 16. Sixteen is the maximum setting for PEEP support to measure the pressure needed to support the lungs during exhale. That day the tears were happy tears. In addition to that, he was able to tolerate oxygen concentration at 70% while maintaining oxygen concentration at 90%; cause for optimism, prayers answered. My prayers are for continuing improvement. God is good.

By now, I know Physical Therapy cannot treat his joints or hands. So, during the rounds, I asked if I could do a passive range of motion. That technique requires manually bending his knees, lifting his arms, bending his wrists and elbows, and moving his shoulders. The answer was yes, as long as I paid attention not to interfere with the equipment. I don't know if it helped Robert, but it sure helped me. I felt like I was doing something to help.

Okay, I knew it when we met; Robert is an avid golfer, playing as many days a week as the weather permits. He enjoys golf outings, watching it on TV, and following his two favorite golfers: Jordan Speith and Scotty Scheffler. On this particular day, the Colonial Golf Tournament was in its final day.

My usual type of communication with Robert was simple, unimportant events of the day, who I had called, who was praying for him, etc., etc., etc. His usual response was no response at all, just stillness. It was okay; my conversations were designed to stimulate his brain and hope for some small response or even a smile. My usual conversations included how much I love him and what the dog was up to, but mostly prayers in hopes that somewhere in his brain he was praying too. During these days, he didn't respond or acknowledge that I was talking to him.

Well, since the final round of the Colonial Open was being televised. I started my usual conversations with a simple, "Hey Babe, the final round of the Colonial Golf Tournament is on at 2:00. Would you like me to turn it on and watch with you?"

His eyes popped open wide, and his head gave a positive yes nod!

I went to the nurses' station where I encountered one of his nurses sitting at the computer. I told her, "I spend hours telling him daily events, stroking his forehead and hair, doing passive range of motion, washing his face with a washcloth and saying things like 'Honey Baby, I love you. I hope you can hear me because I will keep saying it until you wake up.

Well, all it took to get him to respond to my voice was to talk about golf; I think I am going to start making up golf tournaments instead of all the nonsense I have been spewing.

That amazing nurse came into his room and said, "Well if he can respond to that, let's rearrange his room so he can see the screen."

She moved his bed so he could see the screen straight on, instead of off to the side. She knew his eyes were clouded with ointment, but she didn't care, she was dedicated to doing anything to motivate his brain.

She continued to move the heavy ventilator equipment, all the lines connected to the IV stand, and all the equipment meant to sustain his life.

I cannot say enough about her dedication to Robert. In fact, the entire team in the ICU dedicated every moment to Robert's recovery, endlessly and without complaint.

Robert tried to watch the golf match, and since his eyes were covered in ointment to protect his eyes, I served as the commentator.

"Gads, he hit his drive into the rough."

"Great out, he made the green from the rough."

"What a PUTT!"

My commentary lasted a few precious minutes until he fell asleep. I am grateful for those precious moments because they made him happy, even if it was just a few minutes, I knew he was home.

I looked over at the windowsill; the little glass duck was still standing guard.

Chapter 21
The Last 4 days in May 2024
Carol's Point of View

May 28, 2024

The physician's note states: Blinks to threat!

Wait! Blinks to threat means if you move toward his eyes, he will blink. WHAT? That is entirely new; until today, he would just stare, with little or no response, even when the nurse put eye drops in his eyes. Good news indeed.

PEEP 14: Oxygen Concentration at 80%, Oxygen saturation at 90%. Progress! Down from PEEP of 16, and Oxygen Concentration of 100%.

May 29, 2024

He ran a fever overnight, 102. This was the first time his fever was above normal. With the amount of infection in his body, it is odd that he never ran a fever. This is a new development. The doctor changed his antibiotics. Hopefully, this will tackle the fever and whatever infection has emerged.

PEEP score 14, Oxygen concentration 80%. Oxygen saturation 80%-85%. His respiratory status is not improving by much, and with a fever and oxygen saturation percentage well below normal, it isn't a good day.

More prayers, more focus on the positive results from yesterday.

Blood and bone marrow culture:

Preliminary Report

No growth at 1 day. >> Note: Blood and bone marrow cultures will be

continuously monitored for 5 days. A negative report will be generated at

24-hour intervals. If the culture becomes positive an interim report and phone

notification will be issued at that time.

Well, we still don't know what is causing the infection that started this entire illness. Negative culture results have been the result for his entire treatment, and the antibiotics continue to launch an attack on his body in case the bacteria are new and undetectable.

The Nurse Practitioner paid me a visit to discuss palliative care in the event Robert did not recover from his illness. Her note states:

Lengthy DW (Discussion With) Carol, wife at the bedside. She provided additional history and discussed pt's known wishes. Very good understanding of current events and she is well informed. If pt is vent-dependent in the long-term setting, she notes he would not want that QOL. (Quality of Life)

Offered support and discussed that pt will have a protracted recovery.

May 30, 2024

The physician started Lasix today to eliminate fluid accumulation in his body, which causes fluid to leave his body through urine. The physician ordered a culture of sputum and blood, which was extracted through the tracheostomy and PICC line (a permanent needle with multiple ports for staff to administer IV drugs and extract blood for testing) in his right arm.

The most recent chest X-ray indicated Robert was collecting fluid in his left chest X-ray, referred to as a plural effusion, and the physician ordered the removal of fluid in an effort to improve his left lung capacity. A plural effusion will prohibit the lung from fully inflating. If the lung cannot inflate, the oxygen cannot reach the lung's capacity to transfer oxygen to the rest of his body.

The chart states:

> *A time out was performed, and the chest x-ray was reviewed. A preliminary ultrasound evaluation confirmed a LEFT pleural effusion, and the site was marked. The patient was placed in a supine position, and draped in a usual sterile fashion. Lidocaine 1% was used for local anesthesia. A 8 Fr chest catheter was then inserted without difficulty. The procedure was terminated as no fluid aspirated. The catheter was removed while the patient held their breath*

at the end of expiration, and a bandage was placed over the puncture site. A post-procedure chest x-ray is pending. The fluid will be sent for studies, to include: pH, gram stain, culture, cell count and diff, glucose level, protein level, LDH level, cytology, and spun hematocrit.

Findings - 1000 slightly cloudy blood tinged fluid removed

A photo in the record shows a liter of fluid was collected from the procedure.

May 31, 2024

The physician's note states, "1L of fluid removed 5/30". Cultures sent to the lab indicate Cultures of staph epi and cultibacterium. Fluid had leaked from his blood vessels into nearby tissues.

The chart states his prognosis:

Guarded prognosis

Palliative care following, wife reports patient would not want prolonged ventilator dependence. Wants to continue current treatment for now.

PEEP setting 14; Oxygen concentration: 60%; Oxygen saturation 85%-90%

The most positive event of the day is that he can manage with 60% oxygen concentration, he started requiring 100%. Any little step is a step forward to getting off the ventilator.

By now I am coming to the realization that my optimism is serving me well. I have arrived at a place were taking the news one day at a time is best for now, and my prayers continue to ask for total recovery.

The physician began lowering his sedation as a trial to determine if the sedation could be lowered, and he maintained oxygen concentration and saturation levels with less sedation.

I waited anxiously by the bedside for any sign that he recognized me. His eyes were clouded by the ointment and drops necessary to keep his eyes from drying out. Truth be told, the fact that his vision was blurred didn't bother me at the time. I know I didn't look my best; dark circles under my eyes, puffy face from lack of sleep, generally not looking my best.

He spontaneously tried to focus on my face! I leaned over the bed, placed my hand on his hairline, stroked his head, and got as close to his face as possible. "Hi baby, welcome back" I spoke to him with soft, sweet tones. He smiled the first smile I have seen since he died May 19, 2024. He knows who I am! Flood gates opened in my tear ducts; I cried incredible joy right through the tears. "Thank you, Jesus," I whispered, and I knew He heard me because my prayers were answered right there on the spot.

From Robert's point of view:

On the 31st of May, I woke up and opened my eyes to see the love of my life, Carol. She was standing next to me holding my hand and gently brushing my hair off my forehead with her other hand. When she saw I was awake I was treated to the sweetest voice I had ever heard. *Carol said, in the softest, sweetest, most loving tone, I have ever heard, "Hi baby, Welcome back."*

That afternoon, the nurse practitioner noted that the physician had begun to reduce the amount of sedation (Propofol), resulting in increased awareness.

Medical notes:

Drowsy, but wakes easily tracks

Patient has normal respiratory rate and rhythm, FiO2 (Fraction of inspired oxygen) 60, peep 14. Lungs are diminished bilaterally.

Visited with wife, Carol. She states she is very encouraged by patient's improvements, and increased level of alertness today.

I looked out the window, and my little glass duck stood by, steadfast in his job of being the symbol of hope and strength. It may seem silly to assign such lofty duties to a tiny glass duck, but I used him as a focal point for my emotions. I assigned him the duty of being my stolid friend who accepted my emotional roller coaster unconditionally. Today, he shared my joy. I haven't spoken of that little duck to anyone, he was my secret pal.

Chapter 22
1st Week in June 2024
Carol's Point of View
June 2, 2024

Today turned out to be my favorite day…His physician entered room 7, where I was sitting next to Robert's bed, and announced directly, hands on hips, back straight, with a smile on his face: "I AM VERY OPTIMISTIC!"

I burst into silent tears streaming down my face, the relief was immeasurable. For weeks, hope was very dim; he was critically ill, with most staff taking a pessimistic view of his condition, even describing his care as palliative. Until now, optimism from the medical team was supportive for me, but not optimistic about Robert's potential for a full recovery. His medical record entry states:

> *Palliative care following, wife reports patient would not want prolonged ventilator dependence. I explained to her I see signs of improvement and am cautiously optimistic that hoping he will continue to improve with further diuresis.*

> PEEP: 4, Oxygen concentration: 40%

Today, he reached the point where disconnecting the ventilator is a viable option. The Respiratory Therapists are talking about a trial without a ventilator. More tears!

He is beginning to follow simple one-step commands: Lift your arm; can you move your leg? Reach over for the side of the bed. Open your mouth.

Chart entry: "continue weaning/minimizing sedation as able as vent settings improve.

June 3, 2024

Physician's note: *Responding to questions, attempts to interact, weakly phonating and a bit difficult to understand. Wife at bedside very pleased with progress, notes all these changes are new.*

PEEP SCORE: 4. Oxygen Concentration: 30% Still on the ventilator and showing the ability to follow the Respiratory Therapist's directions.

Medical Record entry: *Robert is attempting to answer questions, but he is difficult to understand. He is awake, alert, interactive, orientation difficult to assess. Spontaneously moving all extremities.*

Robert was waking up! He still could not talk; his ventilator was still serving to support his breathing.

Yesterday, I purchased a dry-erase board, marker, and eraser. I elevated his bed so he could write his needs.

The first thing he wrote was: "I died last night".

I could barely make out his writing, his hands were very swollen, and he could barely hold the pen.

The letters were small, almost indistinguishable from chicken scratch.

I spoke his scribble out loud, and he nodded I had read it correctly. He tried to write more but simply could not manage. That little time was an extreme effort, and he fell back to sleep.

I burst into tears. Robert was here; he was aware and tried to send me the most important message of his life, he died and came back.

"Thank you, Jesus, I am a very happy woman today. Thank you for listening to my prayers, I will care for him every day. Thank you, Jesus,".

He slept most of the day, nodding off, waking, and nodding off again.

The Respiratory Therapists discussed the process of turning off the ventilator. They would stay at the bedside with the dials in their hands to see how he did as they lowered the ventilator support.

I was excited and filled with anxiety. "What ifs" flooded my thoughts. I tried to replace my negative thoughts with positive ones, remembering my prayers and asking Jesus to place his hands on the therapist's hands. Faith! Faith! Faith!

June 5, 2024

Today is a trial without the ventilator. That means the Respiratory Therapist will remove the ventilator that has been providing oxygen and pressure to his lungs and see if Robert can maintain adequate breathing without the use of the ventilator.

Robert has a "Trach Collar" in his neck, used to hold the ventilator tubing. The trach collar consists of a firm plastic tube that is inserted into the stoma surgically created at the end of his CPR care. It is held in place by a soft band around his neck. Once the ventilator is removed, the trach collar will be his means of taking and expelling air. It rests inside his windpipe to help him breathe.

The Respiratory Therapists may need to use the opening to conduct emergency resuscitation in the event Robert's breathing is insufficient to keep his oxygen levels at a normal level. He will require a supplemental oxygen supply around the track collar to make sure enough moisture is entering his lungs along with room air and supplemental oxygen. It is like a breathing tube but is held in place in front of the trach tube. It has a flow of moisture mist to help keep the airway moist.

Ok, the appointed time arrived. The Respiratory Therapist, standing next to the emergency supply cart, the nurse and I were anxiously awaiting the second Robert was asked to breathe on his own. 1. 2. 3. GO!

YES! HE IS BREATHING ON HIS OWN!

The Respiratory Therapist asked him to cough. YES, I never thought a cough could sound so sweet. He was able to take in enough breath and cough, which is a major necessity in the event he needs to expel mucous he can.

He tried to talk, but no voice could come yet. The opening is below his voice box. As a Speech Language Pathologist, I learned to read lips, and teach it to people with hearing loss. But that skill had diminished over the years. I tried, I gave it a hard try, and I got a few words, but not all of them. I was certainly able to read his very first attempt at communication. I replied, "I Love You Too Babe".

Robert didn't need any emergency intervention; he was breathing on his own and never looked back. For the first time in weeks, Robert was free from the machines. The only leash he had was IV fluids, giving him sustained fluids and medications.

June 6, 2024

Big day for changes. It's time to hear what he has to say!

When a person has a trach collar, the hard plastic tube keeps the airway open. There is a valve that can be placed on the plastic tube, that allows the patient to talk and be heard. This valve is called a Passy Muir Speaking Valve. It is a small valve with a membrane on the upper edge that vibrates the air moving through it making a sound so he can be understood.

The Speech Language Pathologist arrived in Robert's room early that day to see if he was a candidate for the Passy Muir Valve. She explained to him and me how the valve works, and to be prepared for him to use it for only up to 5 minutes for the first trial.

OK, ready? Robert gave a strong head nod, anxious to be understood.

Snap! The valve was in place.

His first words were, "Hi Babe, I love you". More tears. How many tears can one body create?

Robert started talking and talking and talking. "I died and went to heaven!"

I know you died; you have been in a chemically induced coma for several weeks," I replied.

Robert said, "I know, I saw Jesus, we walked together. I saw my dad. I saw your horses and our dogs."

The Speech Therapist interrupted. "Mr. Marshall, I want you to tell us some important information because you won't be able to tolerate the valve for very long. Are you in pain?"

"No, I am very thirsty, can I have some water?"

"No, I'm sorry, we aren't sure if you can swallow without the water going into your lungs; we have to do a swallow test first."

Robert insisted, "It won't go into my lungs, I know how to swallow!"

Oh boy, this might not be an easy discussion. He is thirsty but since he has been so ill, so debilitated, and had to rely on the ventilator for so long, it is common for swallowing problems to exist. He has had nothing by mouth since May 16th, (22 days). I can only imagine how thirsty he is.

Robert quickly changed the subject, "How long have I been here?"

I replied, "Today is June 6th, you have been here since May 17th. You are in intensive care in Fort Worth."

"Okay, I'm hungry, when can I eat?"

I think he believes if we give him something to eat, it will come with something to drink. He hasn't lost a step!

The Speech Pathologist helped him, "Not until we know you have a safe swallow."

Robert insisted, "I've been swallowing all my life, I am sure I can swallow. Who can't swallow? It's easy; just put it in my mouth; I promise you I can swallow."

Robert continued to talk in that trial session, which lasted for three hours. The nurse was amazed. Most people can only tolerate the introduction of the Passy Muir valve for a few minutes for the first time. Robert asked questions about our friends, our dog, how things were going at home, whether I was okay, and when he could go home…he talked and talked and talked.

He wore himself out, and finally, we removed the valve so he could take a nap.

After his nap, Occupational Therapy and Physical Therapy started their evaluations.

He was very weak and could raise his arm about shoulder high, bend his elbow, and direct his hand to his mouth but could only reach his neck and barely make a fist. She left some stretching bands to encourage him to use them while he was in bed and to try and use them twice more that day.

Physical therapy finished the evaluation. He was unable to sit, it took three of us to hold him to keep him from falling forward or backward. He could not maintain his balance to sit at the edge of the bed. He could bend his knees and flex his ankles, and he promised to keep moving his legs and feet throughout the day.

The Physical Therapist stated, tomorrow she wanted to get him out of bed and into a "neuro chair." The theory is that the more you sit up, the better your breathing becomes.

June 7, 2024

Time to get out of bed. He has been in bed and completely immobile for 23 days. The nurse had the neuro chair brought into his room. It reminded me of a Zamboni seen on ice rinks to smooth ice at hockey games. It was large, with seat belts and high sides to keep him from falling to the sides.

I left the room because it required several strong nurses and therapists to move him safely from the bed to the chair. I was just in the way.

Once he was in the chair, I returned to the room only to hear him clearly commanding the nurses and therapist, "Where's the key? I want to get this thing started so I can go home."

"Robert, there aren't any keys, you are sitting in a chair. There's no engine, no wheels, it's just a chair." Replied the nurse.

"I bet if I get this started, I can get it home! How do I get it started?"

I chimed in, "Babe, we aren't close to home; you are in Fort Worth, and we live 45 minutes from here."

He let me know I was wrong, "No, you are wrong; if I can get through that door (pointing to the hallway), I can get right across that opening and be home in a few minutes."

Oh Boy! Can someone remove the Passy Muir Valve please?

What he had was what is often referred to as ICU psychosis. It is a common occurrence with individuals who have been under sedation, and in the ICU for a long time. And Robert had a good dose of confusion.

After he was discharged and got home, he remembered being in the chair for the first time and thinking his hospital room was on the edge of our community on top of a neighboring barn.

Next to our neighborhood is an equine facility with several horses. Robert believed he was on top of the barn that houses some of the horses.

He remembers being convinced he was only a mile from our house, in fact, he was 45 miles from home.

Chapter 23
June 8, 2024
Carol's Point of View

My phone rang at 8:00 in the morning. It was Robert's nurse, and my heart sank.

"Mrs. Marshall, Robert wants to talk to you, can you talk with him?"

"Of course." I was relieved that he didn't have a setback, nothing is guaranteed during his recovery.

"What's going on?" He shouted. "Where are you?"

"Babe, I am just pulling out of the driveway, I will be there in about an hour." Talking in my most reasonable tone to try to bring some calm to his distress.

"They are taking everything out of my room, they are stealing everything! Make them stop."

"Honey," I replied, "You have been sick for a long time, and now you are much better. You have needed a lot of that equipment in the past, but you don't need it now. Let them take it so someone else can use it to get better."

"Okay, but they are trying to poison me". He insisted, "They want to put stuff in my veins, you have to do something!"

"Ok, Babe, that is your medicine. You have to let them give you your medicine, so you recover enough to come home."

"OK, so you are telling me they have stuff that can help me get home to you?"

"Yes, that's right. Every day, you need to do what they say, and by keeping up with the medicine, it gets us one day closer to getting home."

"OK, I'm going to' trust you, but only because you say so."

Oh boy, today will be one for the record books.

When I arrived, he was sitting with the bed in a full sitting position, and happy to see me when I walked through the door. "I am so happy to see you; please give me a kiss."

He was his usual self. His ICU psychosis appeared to be fading fast.

"I am thirsty, when can I have something to drink?"

I reminded him, "Remember, you have to have a swallow test?"

"I don't need a swallow test, I need water."

"Let me see when it is scheduled." I walked out to the nurses' station to find out when the swallow test was scheduled. "It was for 11:00 today but she moved it to 1:30."

"What did she say?" I told him the news, but he wasn't having it.

"Can I have something to drink while I wait for her?"

"Babe, I am afraid you will aspirate on anything you try to swallow; we don't know how your swallowing will work. You don't want a setback, do you?"

"I can swallow! You don't know how thirsty I am!"

From that second on, no matter who walked through the door, Robert asked, no, begged, for water.

"Can I have a little sip of water? Just a sip?" It was the Respiratory Therapist. "No, I'm sorry, not until your swallow study.

"Can I have just a thimble full of water, just a thimble full?" It was the housekeeper.

"Would you please bring me just one ice chip, just one ice chip? I won't choke, I promise." It was the Chaplain.

This went on all morning, no matter who came to see him, he begged for water.

Finally, after what must have seemed like an eternity to Robert, it was 1:30, time for the swallow study. When the Speech Pathologist entered the room with her equipment, his first comment was, "Oh good, the water truck has arrived!". He asked her, "Can I have something to drink? I am very thirsty, no one around here understands how thirsty I am. Can you bring me a drink?"

She set her equipment on the chair. "I'm here to do just that. I am a Speech Language Pathologist, and I have an intern with me. We are here to do your swallow test."

The swallow test consists of using a thin optical tube with a camera that is inserted into the nose and down the back of the throat to view the vocal cords. The camera allows the therapist to view where food and liquids go during the swallow. If the food reaches the vocal cords, the swallow isn't safe, and the patient is at risk of aspiration pneumonia. If the patient can move food through the mouth and throat to the esophagus and avoid the vocal cords, the likelihood of aspiration is limited, and even avoided.

Robert usually rejects anything going up his nose, but this time he would do anything to be able to get a drink of water. "You know, I don't swallow with my nose, right?"

Since I am a Speech Language Pathologist, the speech therapist permitted me to watch the computer screen during the exam.

First, a graham cracker. Perfect! Next was pudding. Perfect! Next thick liquid. Perfect. And finally, water. PERFECT. Robert's swallow was deemed intact.

Now he can have water! But he had some instructions he had to follow before he would be able to swallow without help.

"First, ALWAYS have the Passy Muir valve in place when taking anything by mouth. Make sure the little bubble at the end of the trach is completely deflated by removing all the air with a syringe. Ask the nurse to double-check it before you put anything in your mouth. Second, take one swallow at a time, no gulping, no matter how thirsty you are. Lastly, keep the Passy Muir valve clean, wash it every time you remove it, and keep it in the container provided. And most importantly, never eat or drink anything without the valve in place." Her instructions were very clear.

Robert said excitedly "Get me some water!"

Chapter 24
June 9, 10 & 11, 2024
Carol's Point of View

June 9, 2024, The big move.

"Mr. Marshall, we are moving you out of the ICU to the Critical Care Unit. You will continue to receive Physical Therapy, Occupational Therapy, and Respiratory Therapy. You are progressing to a lower level of care where your care will continue. We will continue to follow you and your progress."

His physician stated his findings and recapped his progress from ventilator to independent breathing.

I started packing up his medical supplies stored in his room for quick access by the care team. He didn't have any personal items, like clothes, but the equipment was extensive. He will need them in his next room.

I looked directly at the physician, "I will always hold you in high esteem for all the hard work you did day in and day out for Robert. You went the extra mile for him every day; I know it, and I will never forget you, your team, and your efforts. Thank you is not a big enough word to express my gratitude."

Robert was moved to a small room on the Critical Care floor, where one nurse was assigned to four patients. ICU had one nurse for every two patients, so this was a good change, he was a lot more stable.

As soon as Robert left his ICU room most of his ICU psychosis disappeared. It was like a switch turned off. He asked appropriate questions and conversed with the transfer team and nurses accompanying him. Welcome back, Robert!

He settled into his new room and waited for the recovery to continue.

Critical Care June 10, 2024

His first night resulted in an episode of shortness of breath, low blood pressure, and lethargy. The nurses filled me in on the event. Once he was suctioned by the nurse, he had some thick mucus removed during the suctioning, and the issues were resolved.

The physician's note indicates pupils are round, equal, and responsive to light. What a change from his initial condition when he stared straight ahead and could not close his eyelids. There is no more need for the thick ointment used to keep his eyelids moist; he blinks spontaneously and closes them while he is sleeping.

His lungs were clear! Breathing normally! Regular heart rate! Alert, speech slow, no movement disorder noted. The medical record x-ray report stated improved lung function and some remaining congestion in the upper lung regions in both lungs.

When I arrived, he had breakfast in front of him but was only interested in the beverages. He took a few bites and stated he was full.

June 11, 2024

He had another rough night, the supplemental oxygen got disconnected and he felt like he could not breathe. He was frustrated because his Passy Muir Valve was not in; he could not find the call light (it had fallen off the bed), and he couldn't summon help. He eventually threw his cup at the door making a loud bang, but he got help.

When I arrived, he was very frustrated and asked me to find a way to make sure his call light was always within reach. I figured out a way to make the call light in his hand by using a clip to affix it to his pillow. Problem solved.

He ate about 50% of his breakfast and asked for some "home cooking". I made a list for the next day: pudding, yogurt, pimento cheese, V-8 juice.

Time to get out of bed. For the second time, Robert is getting up! It took three people to balance him at the edge of the bed, and three people to transfer him to a neuro chair, but he got there! He sat up for 3 hours that day and enjoyed looking out the window and visiting with me.

Sitting in the chair exhausted him, and he was ready to get back in bed. The same three staff managed to transfer him back to bed. At this time, he had no strength in his legs, so moving him from one surface to the other was extremely difficult. He got into bed, and before the staff left the room, he asked for a favor: "I got my first two legs in bed, can you lift the other two? I am just too tired"

"Your legs are in bed," I told him.

"I know, my first two are, but what about the other two? I want all of my legs in bed, not just these two.'

Oh boy! I thought the ICU psychosis was in our rearview mirror.

"Oh, I see," I stated. "I can help you. Let me lift them for you." I bent over, lifted his invisible legs at the ankle, and placed them carefully next to his legs. Nothing good could come from an argument, it was much better to just do what he asked. This will stay for just a day or two, then like the rest of his confusion, it will disappear all on its own.

I am sure he felt helpless, a new feeling for the man who plays golf, drives and was totally independent before May 17th. After his lengthy illness and dying three times, who could blame him for feeling helpless?

Welcome to Physical and Occupational Therapy!

"It is time to use a walker, Mr. Marshall." The Physical Therapist entered the room with a gait belt and a walker. The idea was to get him to stand and sit. Big order for Robert who had been in bed, immobile for three weeks. The next issue was where to place the gait belt. Without it, the therapist could not control his standing or sitting, with it, it might hit on those very tender broken ribs. She was great, and without hesitation, she positioned the gait belt high under his arms.

OK. 1, 2, 3. Stand up! He got off the bed a few inches and fell back down.

"That's okay, we will try again. Rest for a second."

"OK. 1, 2, 3. Stand up, look up, look at my face. Up, higher, higher. You made it! You are standing." The Physical Therapist was indeed holding him with a strong grip on the gait belt. "OK, now sit down". She lowered him ever so slowly to the bed.

Robert obliged by nearly falling back to the bed, tired and ready to stop. He and the therapist had different plans. She got him to stand again, this time for 5 seconds before he sat again. Progress!

Exhausted, he took a nap.

A few hours later, the Occupational Therapist arrived. "I already had therapy today" complained Robert.

"I know; I am the Occupational Therapist; you worked with the Physical Therapist."

"Well, I am too tired to get out of bed again, can you work with me in bed?"

"Sure, we are going to work on strengthening your arms. You have had quite a rough time since getting here, tell me about it."

The Occupational Therapist had read his chart and knew about his status in Palliative Care. She wanted to know more about how he went from being so ill to now showing the potential for a substantial recovery.

Her idea worked; he didn't think about being tired and worked for almost 30 minutes doing arm-strengthening exercises.

It wore him out, and he needed another nap.

His medical record indicates even more improvement: All of his labs are normal! Amazingly, he went from dead to critically ill and on palliative care to normal labs. God is Great!!

I brought "home cooking," but he wasn't interested; he didn't have an appetite. I visited with the physician on duty who ordered an appetite stimulant to improve his nutrition. His body had a lot of recovery to do, and it couldn't happen without nutrition.

More Physical Therapy, more Occupational Therapy.

June 12, 2024

Today, he stood much better than the first day. He took three steps, alongside the bed. The steps were more like a shuffle, but he stepped. He side-stepped from the middle of his bed to the foot of his bed. AMAZING. It exhausted him, he needed a rest. He had to sit at the foot of the bed for a few minutes, with support to keep him from falling backward. Then he had to use his arm to scoot to the middle before he could lie down. And lie down he did. Exhausted, he took a nap.

Occupational Therapy arrived in the afternoon to resume arm exercises and strengthening. She left some stretching exercises and the bands to use when he practiced while in bed. She reminded him to try to do at least 5 repetitions 3 more times before tomorrow. Guess what, he did it!

Chapter 25
June 12, 2024
Carol's Point Of View

When I arrived that morning, he had breakfast in front of him, and he was trying to eat unassisted. His arm strength and hand strength were now to the point where he could manage a spoon and bend his arm sufficiently to feed himself. I was watching him try to eat a bite of yogurt, and his spoon went directly to his eye. "What the heck?", he asked. I could see he was embarrassed.

"What are you trying to do?" I asked.

"Well, I don't know which mouth is the one that works. I have four arms, four legs and two mouths, but only one of my mouths is working. Which one is the right one?"

"Oh, try the one on the bottom." I offered. "It looks like the one you would use to eat; try that one."

"Okay, let me try that one". And it worked. He aimed lower, "I found the right mouth, the one that is for food, not for talking. The top one is the one I use when I talk". He proudly proclaimed that he figured it out.

Oh boy, it just takes a little longer for the ICU psychosis to work through his mind. He will be fine.

I had to leave the room, so he didn't see me laugh about his predicament.

A Familiar Face

"Hey, you are the guy that broke my ribs!"

A large, tall muscular man walked into his room.

"I saw your name on the patient's list, I couldn't believe it. How do you know who I am?"

It was the nurse who performed CPR on Robert. It was the man who saved his life.

"Because I saw you! I hovered over my bed, I saw you doing CPR on me! I saw the nurses; I saw you breaking my ribs. Then I floated out to the hallway and saw Carol. Then the next thing I knew I was in heaven." Robert was very happy to see this nurse, he knew the hard efforts he exerted to save him.

Robert went on to say, "I came back, and I guess it was you who continued the CPR; I don't know about the other two times. Was it you?"

"Yes", replied our special hero. "Yes, you needed CPR three times; it was me each time; I couldn't give up on you."

Robert Said, "Can I shake your hand?" Tears began to flow out of Robert's eyes, grateful for the man standing in front of him. I wanted to meet you, but I wasn't sure how to find you. Carol said she didn't know who did the CPR because there were so many of you working on me."

"Yes, she was in the hallway, she could not see into the room. We were working very hard to keep you alive; we had the window covered; she didn't know it was me until now."

I cried, Robert cried, and the tissues were spread between us.

"You are not my patient today; I was assigned to this floor today because not too many patients are in the ICU today. When I saw your name, I couldn't believe it. I wasn't sure it was the same person. I had to come to see if it was you. I am very happy to see that you have recovered. I will tell everyone in ICU that I saw you, and you are doing so well."

That man is in our prayers always. We have thanked Jesus for all of the staff, and especially this nurse who tirelessly performed CPR three times and never gave up.

"Look at my beard, do you think I can get a shave?" He found the mirror on his over-the-bed table. Robert's face was beginning to itch. He had not shaved since May 17th and his usual clean-shaven face was a distant past.

A male nurse came to his room, "Sure, I can shave you, I think we have an electric razor; you don't want to try to shave that beard with a safety razor."

"I found our razor, but we don't have the cord. I can't shave you today." The male nurse sounded disappointed; he wanted to make his patient as comfortable as possible.

"No worries, "I stated, I will pick up one on my way home. "I think he would appreciate it."

"More therapy?", Robert exclaimed when the Physical Therapist entered the room. "Don't you know I have been sick?"

"Yes, I know, I am here to make you stronger so we can kick you out!" Her sense of humor motivated him to be an eager participant.

"You know I haven't always been a limp rag; I used to be strong."

She continued, "You took three steps yesterday, what do you think you can do today?"

"Well, I hope I can do three!" joked Robert.

"OK, let's go." She placed the gait belt, helped him stand, and regained his position in a walker, the bed positioned behind him in case he lost his strength and needed to sit down.

OK. Step 1, step 2, step 3, step 4, step 5 around to the foot of the bed.

"I can't, I have to sit!". His knees were giving out.

"Let me take the footboard off; you can just sit on the bed. Stand up for a second, I will hurry." He stood up straight and the therapist removed the footboard off the bed. She tried to ease him to the bed, but he dropped quickly to a sitting position.

"LOOK! He is sitting without someone behind him!", I exclaimed.

"Well, you are getting stronger." The therapist was very pleased with the overnight improvement. "OK, rest a minute, then I want you to walk around the side of the bed so you can get back into bed."

"What? You think I can make it to the other side of the bed?" Robert wasn't so sure.

"Sure, if you just rest for a minute, you can make it," and he did. He rested, walked, and made it.

It was hard, it took strength and perseverance. What started as a goal to take 5 steps ended up with 5 steps twice. Progress. It was progress.

The rest of his stay in the Critical Care Unit was one day of progress after another. He was there for a week when they moved him to a regular room where other patients come to recover from accidents and surgeries.

Chapter 26
Final Days In The Hospital And A New Room
Carol's Point Of View

His new room was spacious with a beautiful view. Physical therapy continued as did Occupational Therapy. He continued to make rapid progress daily until he was strong enough to go home.

He was there for only a few days, therapy continued, his appetite continued, and he lost all symptoms of ICU psychosis.

He was there for only three days when the Chaplain, who had been so kind to me, found her way to his room. She asked if we could walk out into the hall for a brief chat.

"Of course," I stated. We had formed a strong relationship, and I leaned on her for the past four weeks.

"I am so happy to see his progress," she started. "You know, we never see progress like this in the ICU. Most of our patients are too critically ill to have the type of recovery Robert has."

I was as excited as she seemed. Then she continued, "We didn't want to tell you when he was in the ICU, but now it is okay to tell you something that makes his recovery even more remarkable. The entire ICU team gave him less than a one-percent chance of survival, much less than expecting him to make a full recovery like this."

I felt tears stream out of my eyes reaching out for a familiar, comforting hug. I had no idea that the physicians, therapists, and nurses were convinced his condition was so dire. They kept encouraging me, treating Robert as though he were capable of getting out of bed and resuming his prior life.

When we stopped hugging both of our faces were wet with tears. She went on to say, "Our team thinks you are the strongest, kindest, and most loving family member we have ever had the pleasure of knowing. I am so happy we shared these past weeks. I will always remember your willingness to be a part of his care and recovery during his entire time here."

Robert's treating physician walked into his room on the morning of June 18th. After reviewing his medical record, he stated that if the pulmonologist agreed to remove the trach collar, he would be fine planning the discharge.

Later that evening, the pulmonologist's nurse practitioner entered his room and stated, "Let's get that thing out of your neck, so you can go home".

There were some specific instructions:

"Once the trach collar is removed, we will place a gauze over the opening. Every time you talk or swallow, we need you to place your finger over the gauze to direct the airflow up into your voice box and lessen the stress on the gauze. You need to change the gauze every day, and any time it gets soiled. Can you remember to do that?"

"Sure, that seems simple enough."

"Also," she continued, "You will have an open area on your neck for about two weeks, maybe longer, until the opening is completely closed. You will have to keep it covered the entire time until it closes completely."

Standing off to the side of the bed, I committed to reminding him to use his finger to hold the gauze when he talks and swallows.

"Okay, let's get that out of the way." The nurse practitioner removed the string from around his neck, holding the trach tube in place, and in one motion, removed the trach tube that had been in place since May 19th. She cleaned the opening and applied gauze, securely placing the tape on all four sides of the gauze. It was essential to keep debris out of the opening.

"Oh wow, that feels so much better. That thing was causing me to cough, and choke. I can breathe now, without that thing stabbing me in the neck." The look on Robert's face told it all; Prayers answered.

June 19th

That afternoon, the nurse came into the room to change the bandage on Robert's neck.

"Wow, that looks great." She stated. "When did they remove your trach?"

"Last night around 8:00" Robert replied.

"Well, it is already closed. I've never seen one close so fast before. Are you sure it was just last night?"

"Yes, the nurse took it out last night."

"Well, you sure heal fast, there is just a slight opening in the center of the open area. It looks like you won't have much of a scar, if any." The nurse was very surprised at how fast the wound was healing.

Physical therapy worked with Robert, and he could get out of bed and walk with his walker in the room to the sink, to the bathroom, sit on the commode, and walk back to bed. Great progress, he could walk with someone just standing beside him in case he needed some help.

Time to go home.

"I wanted to stop by your room before you left." It was his Pulmonologist from the ICU. "I want to ask you a favor. When you get stronger, and you can walk for longer distances, would you please come up to the ICU and talk to the nurses and doctors? I want all of them to see your progress, we are very excited to see you progress so well." He continued, "You don't have to come to my office, you are done with me. You are discharged from my service."

"I will. I have a lot of people to thank for what you have done for me. I want you to know how grateful I am to you and all of the nurses and respiratory therapists who helped me." Robert was excited to hear that the entire ICU team wanted to see him walk into the unit.

Right before leaving for home, the respiratory therapist came into the room to change Robert's bandage and leave more for bandage care at home. He removed the dressing and exclaimed, "What the heck? I know it has been less than 24 hours, but your wound is completely closed! I have never seen anything like it. All of the edges have met in the middle, you only have a thin line where the stoma is. How can this be? You are a rare patient, sir, this simply does not happen."

He went on to explain that most people who have had a tracheostomy are left with a circular-shaped scar that grows new tissue around the circular opening. He has never seen a tracheostomy scar close in the middle with a thin line.

"Well, I am sending you home. If you see any signs of redness, go to your family doctor for follow-up".

Chapter 27
Welcome Home
Carol's Point Of View

I phoned my neighbors who had been so instrumental in keeping the home front running like a top in my absence. For a month, they had taken care of my dog, mowed my lawn, watered the yard, cleaned my kitchen, and heard every tear roll down my cheeks. They were my every comfort, in the bad times as well as the good times. I know God brought us together for a specific reason; for us to praise God together. And that we did and continue to do today.

When I drove up with Robert in the car, this is what he saw, along with yellow ribbons tied around the trunk of all the oak trees in our yard:

Robert cried like a baby.

He said the sign was special and meant a lot to him. He still has it.

He told me that he had never had a welcome home sign in his life. Even after spending 3 ½ years in Viet Nam. There weren't any welcome home banners when he returned.

Deby and Kevin were by my side unending for the entire time Robert was hospitalized, and continue to be our dearest friends. They are the kind of neighbors everyone dreams of. From the first phone call, until this day, they are amazingly wonderful people who live God's word every day.

During the time Robert was hospitalized, Deby was worried about me and took the time to check on me every day, through phone calls, gifts carefully left in a strategic spot in my home, cleaning up behind me after leaving a messy kitchen on my way out the door and flowers as a surprise to brighten a really tough day.

Kevin mowed my yard several times, (we live on an acre). When I thanked him, his reply was, "No big deal, I just put on my headphones and drive my mower."

Next door to Deby and Kevin live Kevin and Natalie. Yes, two Kevins next to each other. On a very hot summer day, Kevin mowed, edged, and manicured my yard. What can you say about a guy who jumps on his mower and takes care of my yard in 100-degree summer heat? In the front of our yard is a flat concrete curb. Our yard sometimes grows over that flat concrete strip…not under Kevin's watch, he cut away the overgrowth to make my yard perfect.

On the other side of Deby and Kevin live David and Gail. Two newcomers to our neighborhood. Remarkable neighbors who took their turn in caring for the lawn. David jumped on his mower and shared the yard work with the two Kevins.

I am truly blessed to have them as neighbors. I have a neighbor's heart now and will always pay it forward.

I thank God for my neighbors and keep them and their health in my prayers often.

Chapter 28
ALL THE GLORY TO GOD
ROBERT IS HOME
Carol's Point Of View

I was surprised by the banner Deby and Kevin placed on our patio and I didn't expect it.

Before I knew they were planning their banner I had ordered a yard sign for our front yard. I had expected to have it there when we got home, but through some scheduling issues, it was postponed a couple of days.

We were home visiting with Mark, a dear friend of 20+ years when the yard installation of the sign I ordered was taking place. While it was a surprise for Robert, it was an announcement and thanks to all of the neighbors.

This yard sign stayed in our yard for a week, so everyone in the neighborhood knew there was a miracle in our home.

I didn't post anything on the neighborhood Facebook, Robert's condition was dire, and I was hoping no one wanted to visit him in the hospital or send flowers only to have them rejected by the ICU staff.

Since then, the outpouring of good wishes and small gatherings have filled our days with blessings beyond measure. Robert's message has been shared and re-shared with numerous friends and bible study groups.

Spreading his messages from Jesus has taken us to meet new friends and share his story with strangers.

44 HOURS IN HEAVEN, changed our lives.

Chapter 29
A Happy Visit To The ICU
July 9, 2024

I knew we wanted to thank all the Doctors and Medical Staff for all they had done for me during my stay in the ICU and I also had a message from Jesus to give to the Doctors directly.

I also realized that getting all the Doctors, Nurses, Respiratory therapists, Chaplains, and other medical staff together in one group so I could talk to them would be impossible. Getting one Doctor alone in the ICU to talk would be a monumental task. But getting a group of them together that could exceed 25 people, well, let's just say I did not know how that was going to happen.

What I decided to do was write a letter to the Intensive Care Unit Staff and Progressive Care Unit staff to say thank you and to express my deepest gratitude to all the ICU Staff and PCU staff for the exceptional care and dedication they provided during my recent stay in their hospital.

I decided to have the flower bouquets made by my local florist, with the idea that the flowers would be received across all shifts. Too often, discharged patients bring pizza or donuts as a thank you, but that treatment is too short-lived in comparison to the efforts made by the staff who saved my life. They were beautiful white bouquets to signify that they gave me a new beginning.

The flowers and letters were prominently displayed in the break room for each unit.

Now that I could walk well on my own, with the use of a rolling walker, I decided that Carol and I would deliver the flowers and the letters in person. We would take the walker I had used when I first came home because that type of walker had a seat on it. Carol and I picked up the arrangements, and with letters in hand, we started on our way to the ICU. We both felt the same, this trip would be much more enjoyable.

We arrived at the hospital and started the same long walk from the parking lot to the ICU that Carol had made dozens of times while I was in the hospital. Carol knew exactly where the ICU was. Carol knew the distance between the parking lot and the ICU was too long for me to make without sitting for a pause. She was wrong, I made it all the way from the car to the ICU.

As we approached the ICU, the automatic doors opened wide, allowing us to enter directly in front of the nurses' station.

I was pushing the walker with the flower arrangement, and as I entered, I saw a reminder that what I might think is impossible, nothing is impossible for Jesus. *(Luke 18: 27 [NIV])" 27Jesus* replied, "What is impossible with man is possible with God."; (Romans 8:28 [NIV]). "28 And we know that in all things God works for the good of those who love him, who have been called according to his purpose."

With no prior notification on my part, all of the Doctors, Nurses, and Medical Staff were in a group directly in front of the nurse's station.

Carol and I walked in, and I stopped and stood in front of all the Doctors staring at me. It was apparent they did not recognize me and wondered what I was doing there. Carol continued to the nurse's station, putting the flowers and the letter on the counter.

I looked at the Doctors and Medical staff and started the conversation. "You probably do not recognize me, but I am the gentleman who was in Room 7 a few weeks ago. I also am the one who died there three times. What you do not know is I went to Heaven each of the times I died."

I continued, "The third time I died, I went to Heaven I walked and talked with Jesus for 43 hours and 28 minutes. While talking to Jesus, He gave me a message for each of you. I did not know how I was going to get all of you together to give you that message, but now I do."

I proceeded to give them the personal message from Jesus. I was surprised and pleased that every one of them listened intently and tears flowed freely as I gave them the following message:

"Jesus asked me to tell you that he is always present with you when you perform procedures, tests, and direct care for each of your patients. Many times, his hands are on yours as you provide life-giving care.

He also wants you to understand that when someone passes away under your care, it isn't because you did not work tirelessly to save their life, but rather it is time for them to go home. Jesus does not want you to feel like you failed your patients or their loved ones, but rather, you are doing the work he sent you to do."

I then thanked each and every one of them again and told them how grateful I was.

While I was speaking to the group, Carol looked down the hall and saw a familiar face on one of the nurses who cared for me. The nurse approached her, hesitated, and asked, "Oh no, he's not back, is he?"

Carol replied, "He sure is, let me introduce you; I am sure you can't recognize him without the ventilator." Both ladies shared a long embrace, and the tears flowed freely.

"Is that Carol?" came another voice from a patient's room. "Yes, she is here with Robert!"

Before you knew it, nurses, respiratory therapists, and the chaplain all emerged into the hall. Surprised faces expressed joy to see Carol again. Hugs and tears flowed. "I can't believe it!" exclaimed one nurse, and "You are kidding me, that is Robert?" exclaimed another. Phones came out of uniform pockets, and photos were snapped to be shared with the upcoming shifts. Tears turned to joyful smiles and rounds of "Wow, I never thought this day would come."

"Wow, he looks great!" "We didn't give him much hope, he sure fooled us."

Before long one of the nurses interrupted a meeting attended by the ICU Manager. He came into the hallway, saw Carol, and asked if Robert was back. Carol waved her hand toward Robert and said, "Yes, let me introduce you."

The ICU Manager was astonished; his face broke out in a wide smile, and he stated, "I can't believe it. You are walking, you are completely fine!"

"Yes, I am, thanks to your entire ICU team. Everyone from the doctors, nurses, the chaplain, therapists, none of you gave up on me."

The ICU Manager went on to say, "None of us thought you could survive, much less survive like this. Carol was an integral part of our team; she stayed by your side every day and never gave up. I was surprised when she told me you have a Living Will, not many people come here with one. That Living Will gave us a new task; it helped us help Carol. There was a time when I went to talk to her about ending life support, but she wouldn't hear of it. She told me you both agreed to 14 days on the ventilator before making a decision regarding the next steps. We don't see that very often."

Then the nurse who provided CPR walked up to our conversation. "I am glad to see you. The last time I saw you, you couldn't sit up by yourself, much less walk." We hugged, cried, and repeated our unending gratitude for his insistence to continue CPR until the Operating Room Team took over.

Returning to the ICU was the happiest conclusion to a long road and joyful visit to Heaven.

Carol didn't bring the little glass duck home with her; she wanted the next family to have the opportunity to feel what she felt by the presence of that little symbol of strength and perseverance. We peeked into Room 7, and sure enough, the little glass duck was still standing guard.

Epilog:

I am blessed to be alive and healthy.

I fully intend to honor what Jesus commanded me to do in my final conversation with Him in the inner courtyard while sitting on a bench under the canopy of some towering trees on the edge of the River of Life.
Jesus said, "Let Me explain. If you choose to have Me, send you back, I will give you a renewed brain, organs, and body parts that will allow you to function as if you never died. It will enable you to comfort and care for Carol. You will have a complete memory of your life including what I shared and taught you while in Heaven.
"Jesus said, "I command that you share how and why you were allowed to live, as well as what I shared and taught you with anybody that I put in your path. You will entertain any questions about what I shared and taught you from anybody who asks."

Thank you, Jesus, for blessing me with the honor to be your vessel to share your truths, answer questions about you and Heaven and, to convey hope and comfort to all you bring before me.

Questions And Answers While Sharing

The following contains a questions and answers that were asked most often during and after sharing my testimony at various churches, gatherings, and bible study groups.

There are additional questions and answers, that I have posted on the website:
www.44HoursInHeaven.org
www.44HoursInHeaven.com

I also have a section on the website where you can enter your questions. I will answer them and post them on the website.

I look forward to your questions.

Robert@44HoursInHeaven.org

Question:

Does our Love Continue when we die?
Is there Love in Heaven?

The question I was asked in one of our group meetings was whether there is there Love in Heaven. I shared with the person asking the question, that it was actually a question of, "Does our Love Continue when we die?"

There is no question that Love will continue when we die. While in Heaven, I found out firsthand that Jesus is Love. The love that comes from Jesus fills all of Heaven and all that is in it. His Love is in every person, in every tree, in every plant and animal.

Jesus shared with me that Love is the most powerful force in the universe and transcends physical death. Love can heal, unite, and transcend boundaries. It inspires acts of kindness, compassion, and sacrifice. Love is what drives individuals and societies to work together, create beauty, and improve the world. It is a force that resonates with the very essence of our existence.

To understand love and how it transcends death, we must realize that Love is both an emotion and a force. Humanity needs to develop a deep and moving understanding of the relationship between divine love, human connection, and eternal hope found in heaven. The profound truth that God's love is the very essence of heaven must be emphasized. His love is pure, unconditional, and untainted by any negative emotion or experience. This divine love not only fills us in this life but transcends into the life to come, where it will be fully realized in its perfect form.

I learned and would describe love as "the most powerful force there is," transcending even the laws of physics. God's love is a bridge that connects the universe, inspiring and permeating meaning into our existence and helping us transcend ego and isolation while turning to and loving GOD.

Love is not just an emotion but a divine and cosmic force that is the foundation that supports the very structure of existence. God is love and is what all that is good is rooted in. God's love is pure and will bind all true believers to GOD, it underscores love's fundamental nature in Christian theology. *(1 John 4:15,16 [NIV])*, "*15 If anyone acknowledges that Jesus is the Son of God, God lives in them and they in God.16 And so we know and rely on the love God has for us, God is love. Whoever lives in love lives in God, and God in them.*

Love (agape) is the highest expression of God's nature and purpose, through which humanity can achieve salvation and eternal life.

"God's Love and ours should be the same."
(1 John 4:7-21 [NIV]), "7 Dear friends, let us love one another, for love comes from God. Everyone who loves has been born of God and knows God
8 Whoever does not love does not know God, because God is love. 9 This is how God showed his love among us: He sent his one and only Son into the world that we might live through him. 10 This is love: not that we loved God, but that he loved us and sent his Son as an atoning

*sacrifice for our sins. 11 Dear friends, since God so
loved us, we also ought to love one another. 12 No one
has ever seen God; but if we love one another, God lives
in us and his love is made complete in us. 13 This is how
we know that we live in him and he in us: He has given
us of his Spirit. 14 And we have seen and testify that the
Father has sent his Son to be the Savior of the world. 15
If anyone acknowledges that Jesus is the Son of God,
God lives in them and they in God. 16 And so we know
and rely on the love God has for us. God is love.
Whoever lives in love lives in God, and God in them. 17
This is how love is made complete among us so that we
will have confidence on the day of judgment: In this
world we are like Jesus. 18 There is no fear in love. But
perfect love drives out fear, because fear has to do with
punishment. The one who fears is not made perfect in
love.*

*19 We love because he first loved us. 20 Whoever claims
to love God yet hates a brother or sister is a liar. For
whoever does not love their brother and sister, whom
they have seen, cannot love God, whom they have not
seen. 21 And he has given us this command: Anyone who
loves God must also love their brother and sister."*

Love, being the most powerful force in the universe,
speaks to a deep human understanding of connection,
unity, and transformation.

Across time and cultures, love has been revered
as a divine force capable of bridging divides, healing
wounds, and fostering compassion. In this view, love
isn't merely an emotion or experience but a fundamental
energy that holds the power to shape reality itself.

From a Christian perspective, many teachings emphasize love as the essence of divinity. The Bible, for instance, declares, "God is love", (1 John 4:8 [NIV]), "*8 Whoever does not love does not know God, because **God is love***", underscoring love as a supreme and unifying force. The Bible also says that God's love will never die or pass away,

(1 Corinthians 13:1-13 [NIV]) "1 If I speak in the tongues of men or of angels, but do not have love, I am only a resounding gong or a clanging cymbal. 2 If I have the gift of prophecy and can fathom all mysteries and all knowledge, and if I have a faith that can move mountains, but do not have love, I am nothing. 3 If I give all I possess to the poor and give over my body to hardship that I may boast, but do not have love, I gain nothing. 4 Love is patient, love is kind. It does not envy, it does not boast, it is not proud. 5 It does not dishonor others, it is not self-seeking, it is not easily angered, it keeps no record of wrongs. 6 Love does not delight in evil but rejoices with the truth. 7 It always protects, always trusts, always hopes, always perseveres. 8 Love never fails. But where there are prophecies, they will cease; where there are tongues, they will be stilled; where there is knowledge, it will pass away. 9 For we know in part, and we prophesy in part, 10 but when completeness comes, what is in part disappears. 11 When I was a child, I talked like a child, I thought like a child, I reasoned like a child. When I became a man, I put the ways of childhood behind me. 12 For now we see only a reflection as in a mirror; then we shall see face to

face. Now I know in part; then I shall know fully, even as I am fully known.13 And now these three remain: faith, hope and love. But the greatest of these is love.")

Ultimately, we must realize, the reality of love as an "invisible force with significant influence" that impacts our mental and physical well-being, which is uniquely shared by humans, suggests that love is not merely an abstract concept but an inherent quality that defines us. It should remind us that love is a gift from God, a force that, when embraced collectively, can lead to a world characterized by compassion, understanding, and peace. In this way, love is not just a force that affects our individual lives but could be the key to shaping our and others' destinies.

Scientifically, love has been shown to impact our mental and physical well-being significantly. Our brain responds to various stimuli by producing neurochemical messengers called hormones such as **oxytocin, endorphins**, dopamine, and **serotonin.** These hormones travel via the bloodstream to different areas of the body, where they trigger specific functions or feelings.

Understanding that our brain responds to various stimuli demonstrates how love, in its many forms, romantic, familial, or platonic, can affect our health. Beyond happiness, love fosters resilience, helps us cope with stress, and strengthens the social bonds essential for survival.

Love, or lack thereof, is what drives personal and social transformation. Love acts as a bridge between the earthly and the divine, as an agent for self-betterment and growth. Love, having the potential to transcend differences and unite individuals into communities, speaks to its civilizing power.

The reality of love's interconnectedness transcends death and resonates with the emerging views in science that everything in the universe is deeply interconnected. Love must be understood as a force that resonates with this interconnectedness, playing a role in the unseen bonds that link consciousness, energy, and matter.

Love is the most powerful force in the universe and resonates with a profound universal truth of interconnectedness. Though often viewed as an intangible concept, perspectives and evidence demonstrate love's transcendent and transformative power with its potential as a unifying force.

Knowing that love never dies and transcends death gives us the comforting thought that those in Heaven are enveloped in God's love and are free from death, pain, sorrow, or worry. It speaks to the promise of heaven as a place of complete peace and joy.

While our loved ones are not able to look down on or intervene in our earthly lives directly, God's love is the bridge that continues to connect us to our loved ones who have died. It gives us assurance and comfort knowing that they are in heaven because we still have that connection through the love of God. It also assures us that we have God's love in us because a corrupt and cursed human love would not transcend death, and the connection via God's love, would not be there. The memories, dreams, and experiences we have of our loved ones are indeed real, but they come through the comfort of God, reminding us of the unique eternal connection we share through His love.

This understanding encourages us to rejoice in the knowledge that our loved ones are in a place of peace and love, and that we, too, will one day join them in God's eternal embrace.

The reassurance that we are still connected to them through God's love is a source of great comfort, especially during moments of grief or longing. Understanding this also provides hope, not just for the future reunion in heaven but for the peace we can experience here and now, knowing that God's love continues to bind us together.

True love is not merely physical but also intellectual and spiritual, a force that drives us toward the good from God's Love, patience, kindness, truth, trust, and hope. It can also be said that love is the force that elevates us from the material realm to higher spiritual truths. Similarly, love fuels the quest for wisdom and virtue, uniting the body and soul to pursue the ultimate good and God. *(1 Corinthians 13: 4-7 [NIV]), 4Love is patient, love is kind. It does not envy, it does not boast, it is not proud. 5It does not dishonor others, it is not self-seeking, it is not easily angered, it keeps no record of wrongs. 6Love does not delight in evil but rejoices with the truth. 7It always protects, always trusts, always hopes, always perseveres.)*

The evidence suggests that love's influence extends far beyond personal relationships. Love is a biological necessity for humans, an ethical compass in philosophy, a central tenet in spirituality, and a form of clarity for identifying the hidden force responsible for the universe's interconnectedness. While science may not quantify love as a physical force, its effects on our lives are undeniable, uniting us, fostering empathy, and leading to growth. Love remains the most powerful force in shaping our emotional, spiritual, and societal evolution.

The opposite of love is not envy, boastfulness, pride, dishonoring others, self-seeking, easily angered, keeping a record of wrongs, or delighting in evil or maliciousness. These are traits that love is not.

The opposite of love is the part of us that asserts our free will independently without concern for God's love being the guiding force to experience individual freedoms.

When we exercise our free will and make choices or decisions without love being the prevalent guiding factor in our free will, we are being guided by the characteristics or traits that God's love is not. When we do so despite God's love that we have in us, is the reason and when we sin.

In many ways, free will makes us our own worst enemy. When it comes to what love is not; love is not envious, boastful, prideful, dishonoring others, self-seeking, easily angered, keeping a record of wrongs, or delighting in evil or maliciousness. It is when we abuse or corrupt our free will and exercise our ability to choose with wrong motives and reasons that can lead to conflict, hatred, and the perpetuation of these negative emotions and actions. It allows us to hold grudges, seek revenge, and build barriers between ourselves and others, causing conflicts among ourselves, others, and nations worldwide.

Love is the foundation of society, influencing and causing cooperation, empathy, and a sense of belonging. On the other hand, the absence of love can lead to isolation, division, and discord. Thus, I believe that by conforming ourselves to love, Through mindfulness, kindness, or spiritual practice, we can achieve a more harmonious existence, both individually and collectively. *(1 John 4:8 [NIV*]).* "God is love", "*8 Whoever does not love does not know God, because* **God is love,**"

Question:
Can our loved ones look down on us after they passed?

Let me share with you the reality of how love's interconnectedness transcends death and resonates with the emerging views in science that everything in the universe is deeply interconnected. Love must be understood as a force that resonates with this interconnectedness, playing a role in the unseen bonds that link consciousness, energy, and matter.

Love is the most powerful force in the universe and resonates with a profound universal truth of interconnectedness. Though often viewed as an intangible concept, perspectives and evidence demonstrate love's transcendent and transformative power with its potential as a unifying force.

Knowing that love never dies and transcends death gives us the comforting thought that those in Heaven are enveloped in God's love and are free from death, pain, sorrow, or worry. It speaks to the promise of heaven as a place of complete peace and joy.

While our loved ones are not able to look down on or intervene in our earthly lives directly, God's love is the bridge that continues to connect us to our loved ones who have died. It gives us assurance and comfort knowing that they are in heaven because we still have that connection through the love of God. It also assures us that we have God's love in us because a corrupt and cursed human love would not transcend death, and the connection via God's love, would not be there. The memories, dreams, and experiences we have of our loved ones are indeed real, but they come through the comfort of God, reminding us of the unique eternal connection we share through His love.

This understanding encourages us to rejoice in the knowledge that our loved ones are in a place of peace and love, and that we, too, will one day join them in God's eternal embrace.

The reassurance that we are still connected to them through God's love is a source of great comfort, especially during moments of grief or longing. Understanding this also provides hope, not just for the future reunion in heaven but for the peace we can experience here and now, knowing that God's love continues to bind us together.

Question:
What will we look like in Heaven?

Jesus explained to me that we will be ageless yet have various physical appearances. At first, there will be children and adults in appearance because there will be no chronological age as we experience now.

As heavenly beings, we will possess both the vigor of youth and the wisdom of maturity. Agelessness is the eternal nature of existence in Heaven and the New Earth, where time, as we understand it, does not pass or affect us in the same way. All people entering Heaven will receive a perfect physical body.

Agelessness and physical age are no longer defining or limiting factors in Heaven and the New Earth because there is no more death, mourning, crying, or pain; we will be ageless yet have various physical appearances of chronological ages.

All persons who died as adults who have not reached their chronologically physical age of perfection will either continue to grow and mature or revert back to their chronologically physical age of perfection. If you, for example, died as a teenager, you would continue to grow, or if you are older, you will revert back.

In Heaven, the imperfections and limitations of our earthly bodies will no longer apply. Instead, people will experience a state of perfection, where our bodies transcend the cycles of aging, disabilities, deformities of any kind, decay, or frailty that we are familiar with on Earth.

Scripture states, *"Revelation 21:1-4, [NIV])*
1 Then I saw "a new heaven and a new earth," for the first heaven and the first earth had passed away, and there was no longer any sea. 2 I saw the Holy City, the new Jerusalem, coming down out of heaven from God, prepared as a bride beautifully dressed for her husband. 3 And I heard a loud voice from the throne saying, "Look! God's dwelling place is now among the people, and he will dwell with them. They will be his people, and God himself will be with them and be their God. 4 'He will wipe every tear from their eyes. There will be no more death or mourning or crying or pain, for the old order of things has passed away.

"While we may retain adult appearances, our hearts, and spirits could be marked by the wonder and lightness of children, living in a harmonious and renewed creation. The image of eternity where childlike wonder meets mature understanding paints a picture of deep fulfillment and peace, aligning with the idea of eternal joy in God's presence.

These reflections encapsulate the hope and mystery of what awaits believers in Heaven and the New Earth. The emphasis on perfection, joy, and vitality, as well as the idea that relationships will be transformed and deepened by the fullness of God's love, is comforting and reassuring peace. It acknowledges our wonderment of the unknowns while focusing on the promises of Scripture about the beauty and completeness of eternal life in God's presence.

Question:

What happens to babies that are stillborn or aborted, or die within a short period of time after birth?

This was a question I am happy to share how Jesus explained it to me.

At first, there will be children and adults in appearance because there will be no chronological age as we experience now. The appearance of a child in Heaven and the New Earth will be that of the age of the child when they died. In the case of a stillborn or aborted baby, they will be that of a newborn. The child will mature slowly, physically and spiritually, until reaching their individual age of perfection.

Jesus shared with me that children are not held accountable by God for their sins until they reach a certain age. If a child is aborted, or the mother suffers a miscarriage, or the child is stillborn, that child will, by the grace and mercy of God, be granted entrance to heaven as a newborn baby.

However, once a child is born, if he or she should die before reaching their individual "age of accountability," that child will, also by the grace and mercy of God, be granted entrance to heaven.

Jesus does all things out of Love, and His handling of the early separation of child and mother is no different. Jesus said that when a mother dies and enters heaven, her child will be waiting for her. She will still have the same relationship of mother-daughter or mother-son of the child who died earlier.

In heaven, parents will have restored, the love and joy that they never were able to experience, watching their child grow up and mature to the age of perfection and do so in an environment of perfect peace, joy, and righteousness of Heaven and the New Earth. This should be an extremely comforting thought for parents who have lost children at an early stage of life.

Jesus pointed out that His death was sufficient payment for the sins of all of mankind, including the whole world. We are to remember that the entire world is under the curse of sin, including animals, plants, trees, and every living creature

Jesus pointed out that His death was sufficient payment for all sins, not only the sins of those who come to Him in faith. The fact that His death was sufficient for all sin allows God to apply that payment to those who were never capable of believing or never had the opportunity.

Question?
What constitutes a miracle?

The scriptural definition of a miracle is an event involving God's powerful and direct action, transcending the standard laws of nature and defying expectations of behavior. Miracles are remarkable occurrences that can only be attributed to God's supernatural work and show His involvement in human history. In the Bible, God uses miracles to reveal His character, Himself, and His purposes to humanity through phenomena that aren't otherwise explainable.

All the books in the world couldn't record the miracles that Jesus Christ did. Healing the blind. Walking on water. Calming the storm. Feeding thousands with a few loaves and fish. Every miracle Jesus performed was for a purpose. He performed thousands of miracles to show us that God is real, God loves us, and God wants to heal and restore us to abundant life.

The miracle you need most in life will lead you to what you really need most, a deeper relationship with God. Our relationship with our Heavenly Father is so important. Miracles draw us closer to Christ because they always reveal Jesus' character. Oftentimes, when we think about or study the miracles of Christ, we only look at the wow of the miracle, and we miss the wonder of God's character. Luke 4:40-41 is a great example of this. The Bible speaks of Jesus' healing in these verses. If you read the short passage quickly, your takeaway may simply be that Jesus cast out demons, but if you read deeper, you'll see that Jesus attended to people individually. He touched each one. He made it personal. The miracles of Jesus draw us closer to Him.

Most believers today can acknowledge God's ability to heal. But like the leper who came to Jesus in Matthew 8 begging for healing, they pray, "If it be your will Lord, heal me." They are just not sure that it is God's Will for them to be healed. It's important that we remember that God's promises are timeless. When you bring your need to the Lord in prayer, take the "if" out of your asking and pray in faith, expecting to receive. It is God's Will for you to walk in divine health and be in the right relationship with Him. Just as it was when the Lord Jesus walked this earth, signs, wonders, and miraculous acts still occur today.

God does miracles His way, and it's often when people don't expect them. You might be sitting by the edge of a pool looking for assistance, healing, or an escape from your circumstances. In that moment, Jesus may do something you never thought or imagined He'd do. This was the case with the paralytic. Jesus asked the man, "Would you like to get well?" and the paralytic man said to Jesus, "I can't, sir, for I have no one to put me into the pool when the water bubbles up. Someone else always gets there ahead of me." As he begins to talk to Jesus, he starts to experience some hope. He sees his deliverance in the Bethesda pool, but instead, Jesus tells him, "Stand up, pick up your mat, and walk." Jesus didn't need a healing pool, magic, or troubled waters. At that moment, he was telling the paralytic that He was the miracle. The same goes for us. We don't need to look towards people or things as the solution that will change our lives. Jesus is the miracle and has the power to transform us.

If you are ready for a miracle to occur in your life, your faith must be in God and in His Word, not in your own or someone else's spiritual gift. The apostle John wrote, "*1 John 5:14,15. "This is the confidence that we have in Him, that if we ask anything according to His will, He hears us. And if we know that He hears us, whatever we ask, we know that we have what we asked of Him."*

We understand through these verses that we can have faith in that which we ask, "according to His will." There is no point in trying to convince ourselves that something must be His will or hoping hard enough, refusing to allow any doubts to enter into our minds. We can know that anything God has promised or commanded is according to His will. Beyond that is up to God to give us certainty and faith in any particular case.

God can and does miracles for people today because of His incredible love for us. It was the same in the Bible times: *"Luke 6:19 The whole multitude sought to touch (Jesus), for power went out from Him, and healed them all."* But the ones who saw miracles every day were those who were with Him all the time. Rather than living our own lives, ignoring Jesus, and then coming to Him when we need a miracle, we should enter into a close personal relationship with Him, following Him every day. When we do this, we will see the greatest miracle of all, as our life changes to become like His.

There are hundreds of accounts of miraculous healings today among countless Christians. God miraculously heals some while choosing not to heal others for His divine purpose. No one could accuse the apostle Paul of having a weak faith, yet God refused to heal Him after he asked Him three times. God knows who and what to heal and what is best for the believer in choosing not to heal someone. God's higher wisdom is always at play. Remember, these are at the discretion of God alone. Trust in His decision-making, even if the outcome isn't what you expected or when you wanted it. Our sufferings and afflictions work out a purpose that we may not be able to understand at the time.

Question:

What is Free Will?

Our free will and the power to choose are both a blessing and a burden. It is the source of our most outstanding achievements and our gravest mistakes.

In this world, where love is meant to be the prevailing force, the contradicting nature of free will presents itself. While free will is a unique and precious gift, it is also a double-edged sword. It allows individuals to make choices that either nurture and enhance love or block and undermine it.

Our free will allows us to make decisions that are not always aligned with love. It enables individuals to prioritize their self-interest, leading to actions that can hurt others and create division. It can breed selfishness, cruelty, and the pursuit of power at the expense of love and compassion.

Balancing Love and Free Will is a challenge for humanity. We have to strike a balance between the gift of free will and the power of love. While free will gives us the capacity to make choices that block love, it also allows us to choose love. Love requires conscious, intentional choices. Love asks us to use our free will to overcome our own worst tendencies and ultimately to God's Love.

The *uniqueness* of free will as both a hindrance and a promoter of love is a unique challenge for humanity. It is up to everyone to use their free will in ways that align with the universal force of God's love and to choose empathy, compassion, and unity over hatred, division, and selfishness. By doing so, we can harness the immense potential of free will to overcome its inherent contradictions and allow the power of love to prevail in our lives and the world. Love is the most powerful force in the universe, and when used wisely, our free will can amplify its transformative impact.

Love is so powerful, and yet it fails to eradicate narcissism (the free will choice to be cruel, selfish, and manipulative without regard for the well-being of others). We can be sure that God's love is pure and strive to live according to His love and desires.

Question:
Will our Pets be in Heaven?

I am happy to say absolutely! Yes!

Those who read the book "44 HOURS IN HEAVEN" already know the answer and why I am so sure. For those who have not had the chance to read the book, I am excited to share how and why my answer is yes.

On May 19th, 2024, I died 3 times and went to Heaven each time I died. When I died the 2nd time, I went to Heaven instantly. Just like the first time I went to Heaven, I experienced the love and peace, the beauty, the smells in the air, and the feelings of being connected to everything and everyone and they were a welcoming familiarity of coming home.

Unlike the first time, I was standing at the edge of a beautiful field of tall grass that had the same beautiful trees scattered throughout. Looking to my left, in the far distance, I saw the inner courtyard and my dad was still there, but this time, my mom was there.

I looked around, still in amazement at how beautiful everything was, how magnificent and bright the colors were, how warm and loving the light, sounds, and smells that filled the air were, and how peaceful and calm it was.

It was at this time I was treated to a surprise. Our pets that we love are in heaven!

Two horses and three dogs greeted me. The horses were Carol's and mine; their names are Shakush and Nugget.

Shakush is a pure white Arabian who has the personality of a playful clown. He would get in the arena without Carol on his back and jump and play with her like a playful dog would do, except he was a horse and much larger, but just as gentle. Carol raised and trained Shakush herself and was the only person who rode him. Carol was and still is an excellent horseperson and rider. She glides when riding, and it is a thing of beauty to watch. When Carol and Shakush were both younger, she would show him at horse shows, and they often finished in the top 3. When Carol would ride him, he was always a perfect gentleman, and they would ride for hours in the arena and open fields. While running uphill on a trail he would buck, tossing his head in absolute joy. Regardless of the hill, the gait, or his mood, Carol could always brace herself for a joyful exuberant buck.

Nugget is a buckskin quarter horse and absolutely beautiful. She did not have the same personality as Shakush, but rather, she always acted very regal and gentle. Carol would ride Nugget, and on a rare occasion, she would share Nugget with me for a trail ride. Nugget was raised and trained by Carol just like Shakush. Both Shakush and Nugget were magnificent horses and were truly a gift and blessing from God.

Three dogs greeted me with our two horses. Two of the dogs that greeted me are named Fudge 1 and Fudge 2 because they are dark brown and sweet, just like Fudge. We named all of our dogs Fudge, so we don't get their name wrong when a new pet joins our family. There was a third dog that approached me in Heaven with the others, but I did not recognize her. I later learned the dog was named Annie and was Carol's dog before we met.

Fudge 1 was a rescue dog that was a sweet little dog that would run and play his game of catch me. Of course, it was only when he decided to let us catch him that we were able to. Then he would cuddle up like the sweet dog he was. It was his way of playing.

Fudge 2 was used as a bait dog prior to our rescuing him. He wanted to be sweet and loving but had some prior issues as a result of his abuse before he became part of our family. There were times he would snap or have a flashback. It took a long time and a lot of love before he would trust us. However, he eventually did, and he turned out to be a sweet little boy. He would jump around like a kangaroo. He was unbelievably quick and would spring around like a bouncing ball. He still had flashbacks occasionally, back to when he was abused and treated so meanly. When this happened, it was as if he recognized what happened and was sorry for snapping at us, that was when we got the most loving and cuddling from him. Our best efforts did not erase his abuse on earth. In heaven he's no longer like that. He is a happy puppy running and playing.

The third dog's name was Annie. I didn't know the third dog's name until I was out of the hospital and was telling Carol about going to Heaven and our pets being there. It was when I described the dog I did not recognize that she said it was her dog, Annie. Carol had Annie before I even knew her. Mystery solved.

We currently have a dog, and of course, that is Fudge 3. He is a spitting image of Fudge 2, only sweeter.

So, when I say that our pets are in Heaven, it is not just a hopeful desire; it is an eyewitness account. I saw our horses and dogs, and they were as happy as they could be, waiting for us to come home.